PENN HIGH SCHOOL
INSTRUCTIONAL MATERIALS CENTER
MISHAWAKA, INDIANA

DISCARD

Who Cares?

MILLIONS DO...

Who Cares? MILLIONS DO . . .

A BOOK ABOUT ALTRUISM

Milton Meltzer

WALKER AND COMPANY NEW YORK

Copyright © 1994 by Milton Meltzer

All rights reserved. No part of this book may be reproduced or transmitted in any form or by any means, electronic or mechanical, including photocopying, recording, or by any information storage and retrieval system, without permission in writing from the Publisher.

First published in the United States of America in 1994 by Walker Publishing Company, Inc.

Published simultaneously in Canada by Thomas Allen & Son Canada, Limited, Markham, Ontario

Library of Congress Cataloging-in-Publication Data
Meltzer, Milton, 1915–
Who cares? : millions do— / Milton Meltzer.
p. cm.
Includes bibliographical references.
ISBN 0-8027-8324-4 (cloth).—ISBN 0-8027-8325-2 (reinforced)
1. Altruism—Case studies—Juvenile literature. 2. Volunteers—United States—Juvenile literature. 3. Voluntarism—United States—Societies, etc.—Directories. [1. Altruism. 2. Social action. 3. Voluntarism.] I. Title.
BJ1474.M45 1994
171'.8—dc20 94-4082
CIP
AC

Book design by Ron Monteleone

Printed in the United States of America

2 4 6 8 10 9 7 5 3 1

Let no one be discouraged by the belief that there is nothing that one man or woman can do against the enormous array of the world's ills, against misery, ignorance, and injustice. Few will have the greatness to bend history itself; but each of us can work to change a single portion of life's events, and in the total of all those acts will be written the history of this generation. It is from numberless diverse acts of courage and belief that human history is shaped. Each time a man stands up for an ideal, or acts to improve the lot of others, or strikes out against injustice, he sends forth a tiny ripple of hope and crossing each other from a million different centers of energy and daring, those ripples build a current which can sweep down the mightiest walls of oppression and resistance.

—ROBERT F. KENNEDY

Contents

Foreword

It's hard to read or see the news without learning how greedily and selfishly some people act. Even those who seem to have everything want more. Their wealth and their power are never enough.

No surprise, say many editorials. Aren't such people the product of a culture that glorifies materialism, individualism, competition? To them, "making it" is everything. They measure their worth by the number of dollars they pile up or the size of the deals they make. "Looking out for Number One" invariably means others get stepped on. No wonder many cross over the line of legality and decency and are found guilty of corrupt practices.

Not long ago when a Texas politician was accused of corruption he replied, "Why you pickin' on me? Ever'body does it."

But do they? Is it true?

Or is there another side to American life to which all too little attention is paid?

Who Cares?

MILLIONS DO . . .

1 Heroes—and Ordinary People

This is a book about that other side of American life.

Altruism, it's called.

It means a concern for and devotion to the interests of others. It's commonly used as the opposite of egoism, or selfishness.

A word confined to the dictionary, sniff the cynics. But in real life, here and now? What place does altruism have? Who cares about anyone but "me"?

Lots of people do. More than 105 million Americans volunteer an average of four hours a week to help causes or individuals. Of this number, 98 million are adults, and nearly 8 million are fourteen- to seventeen-year-olds. The value of their volunteer time is estimated at $174 billion a year. But you can't put a dollar sign on their worth; it's priceless.

Perhaps the most dramatic example of unselfish behavior is the hero or heroine. They are the people we honor because of their exceptional service to humankind. They help others when there is no possible gain for themselves. In fact, their courageous deeds often place their own lives in jeopardy.

We've read about great heroes of the past in world literature, in the romances and epics of many cultures. Everyone knows about the Congressional Medal of Honor awarded for extraordinary heroism in wartime. But there are men, women, and children in time of peace who also act to rescue their fellows. Here are just a few of them:

- Derek Lambert, sixteen, of Andrews, South Carolina, who saved a man who had fallen from a boat and severely cut his hands on the propeller.
- Michael B. LaRiviere, eighteen, of Rockaway, Oregon, who died while swimming to save a man caught in an ocean current.
- Jerry L. Conrad, thirty-five, of Toledo, Ohio, who leaped into a moving car to save a three-year-old girl.
- Allen N. Davidson, thirteen, of Gaffney, South Carolina, who crawled into a burning house and dragged an elderly woman to safety.

These examples of heroism are taken from the lists of people honored each year by the Carnegie Hero Fund. It recognizes outstanding acts of selfless heroism performed in the United States and Canada. Established in 1904, it

Mark White, a seventeen-year-old high school student, was awarded the Carnegie Medal of Honor for saving Sally Swanson *(right)* from drowning in Santa Clarita, California, in 1992. *(Kevin Karzin/The Signal AP Leafdesk)*

has honored nearly 7,500 North Americans since that time.

We know of course that even heroes are not perfect. It's almost certain that none of those awarded Carnegie Medals were without weakness or blemish. Heroes are often "ordinary people who somehow manage to do extraordinary things," as the writer Madeline L'Engle has pointed out. "The heroic personality is human, not perfect, but human. And to be human is to be fallible." If you trace heroes through literature and legend and history, you see how often heroes make terrible mistakes. What matters is their ability to stretch themselves beyond their limitations at times of crisis.

This gives the rest of us hope. Maybe we can do it, too. The seed of altruism is within ourselves, wanting to spring forth and grow.

There is more than one kind of heroism. What the Carnegie Medal singles out are the emergencies that involve threat of harm or actual harm, and the selfless heroism of people who come to the rescue.

What about the people who express their altruism in social action, and do it daily? They are able to identify with others—in need, in trouble, in danger—to do what many of us are afraid to do, fearing the threats and sacrifices that come with commitment to others.

Mother Teresa is an example recognized and admired the world over. The Yugoslavian nun has worked more than forty years among the desperately poor of Calcutta, India. She founded the Roman Catholic Missionaries of Charity who live no better than the poor among whom they work in dozens of countries. Mother Teresa and her coworkers do not try to convert others. They simply tend "the poorest of the poor," to live out, as she says, "that life of love, of compassion, that God has for his people." To her the rights of others not only matter as much as her own but matter even more, in a true spirit of selflessness.

The same spirit emerges from the pages of our pre–Civil War history. We read of abolitionists who devoted their lives to the struggle to end slavery. Some of them, at great risk, went into the South to rescue black people from bondage. Perhaps 2,000 slaves a year escaped from their masters, most of them through their own ingenuity and daring. Many fugitive slaves, however, were helped to freedom by African-Americans or by whites. Harriet Tubman, born into slavery in Maryland, ran away to freedom at the age of twenty-nine. Working as a domestic in Pennsylvania, she managed to save enough money to finance periodic trips to the South to rescue family and friends. Sometimes she carried infants and even exhausted men to freedom. She made nineteen of these dangerous trips, freeing, she estimated, more than 300 slaves. During the Civil War, in her early forties, she served in South Carolina for three years as a spy, scout, and nurse for the Union army. She lived into her nineties.

One of the white "conductors" on the Underground Railroad was Calvin Fairbank. Born in upstate New York in the early 1800s, he became a circuit preacher on the frontier while still a youngster. Gradually he moved

Harriet Tubman escaped from slavery but returned to the South nineteen times to rescue 300 slaves. She stands on the left, with her husband seated near her, and with a group of her "passengers" on the Underground Railroad. *(Schomburg Center for Research in Black Culture)*

toward abolitionism. One day he decided to do more than preach against slavery among Northerners. He would identify himself with the black people "that are in bonds as bound with them." So he crossed the Ohio River into Kentucky. It was in this slave state that most of his daring rescues took place. He helped dozens of slaves reach free soil. He was caught twice and sentenced to prison each time, serving a total of seventeen years behind bars.

More than a hundred years later another group of Americans, black and white, like Tubman and Fairbank, went into the South again. This time their mission was to register African-Americans to vote. Using local ordinances, threat of job loss, and violence, white racists had succeeded in preventing most blacks from exercising their right to register and vote. For though the Civil War had ended slavery, it did not end discrimination and segregation. Black people still lived in poverty and were oppressed. They seemed free in name only. Jim Crow laws narrowly restricted their lives. Even their participation in the U. S. armed forces that helped win victory over Hitler's Nazi system in World War II did not change many things for African-Americans.

Then in 1954 the Supreme Court's *Brown* v. *Board of Education* decision revolutionized American education. The court declared that separate schools for blacks and whites were unconstitutional, and called for an end to segregation. When the legal barriers fell in education, a dream was rekindled in the heart of black America—to live in a nation where all people were treated equally and were not judged by the color of their skin. In the 1950s blacks began the modern civil rights movement to make that dream become a reality. Activists used boycotts, sit-ins, freedom rides, picketing, and mass marches to advance the cause.

One of the organizations founded to speed victory was the Student Nonviolent Coordinating Committee (SNCC). Its objective was to promote integration in the South. In 1964 SNCC conducted the Mississippi Summer Project, hoping to bring about changes in that most backward of states through black voter registration and education. SNCC volunteers included about 1,000 northern students, lawyers, doctors, ministers, and teachers, from all over the country. About half were young whites, many of them of upper-middle-class background. They underwent intensive training on an Ohio campus and then went down to Mississippi to begin their work.

They organized fifty freedom schools and established another fifty community centers.

That summer in Mississippi the unprovoked killing of African-Americans multiplied and went unpunished. There were over 1,000 arrests of the young freedom volunteers. Thirty were wounded by gunfire, and three young organizers—James Chaney, Andrew Goodman, and Michael Schwerner—were murdered by white terrorists.

What made these young men and women volunteer in the face of such dangers? Religious values? Secular values? A spirit of adventure? "All of these," suggests the Harvard psychiatrist and author Robert Coles, who interviewed many of them, "and maybe any number of idiosyncratic motives."

One of the voter registration volunteers that summer was Michael Yarrow, a young white man. He had been born in Mississippi where his father had a one-year teaching position at the state university. The family later returned to the North. After the orientation session in Ohio in 1964, Yarrow, then a Queens College student, reached Mississippi and was taken into the home of an elderly black couple, the Shields, in the town of Ruleville. From the letters he wrote his family and friends, we can get a good idea of what he did and saw that summer. Here's the first of a number of excerpts:

> *Just the precautions [in Ohio] are scary: beware of cars with tags, they are always dangerous; never go out alone; never go out after dark; never be the last out of a mass meeting; watch for cops without their badges; listen for an accelerating car outside; turn off the globe lights and tape the door lights on your car; if you wake up at night thinking there is danger, wake everybody up. (There seems to be an instinct for self-preservation.) The Negro civil rights workers from Mississippi told how they played like real Uncle Toms to the cops when in real danger. They advised us to play like Northern kids just come down to see how things are, to say we had read all this stuff in the Northern press and couldn't believe it. They stressed the importance of sticking together—going to jail together, taking the blows for someone else.*

He was scared from the first night he slept in the Shields' home and saw that they locked his bedroom windows. In the morning he realized his fears connected him with people who had lived in fear all their lives. They—and he—had intensely personal reason to be fearful, for the three civil rights workers—Chaney, Goodman, and Schwerner—had just disappeared. No one yet knew for sure that they had been murdered. Again, Yarrow writing home:

> *These people live under the almost absolute power of the white community. This relieves the whites of most of the external limits to their use of power. As the Negro community becomes united in its determination to stand up, it becomes much harder for Negroes to be pushed around. Perhaps one of the most exciting things about this town is the way Negroes talk to us or wave to us in full view of their employers or the police.*
>
> *But even with the strong movement that is growing in Ruleville, justice seems far off. One man told me that he hasn't been able to get compensation from the railroad even though he had been totally disabled for six years. Others have been fired or taken off social security for registering to vote. The lady next door was told by the mayor that she might be beat up if she took in some freedom workers. Recently three field workers were killed when they fell off an overloaded truck coming back from the fields. A state trooper told the director of our project that if he had a chance he would grind him into the dirt like a bug. When the mayor came around to investigate the shooting into three houses a year ago where SNCC workers were*

staying, he said he wished they had got a whole bunch of them niggers.

The project leader in Sunflower County was Charles McLaurin. Yarrow found him to be a dynamic speaker whose determination, good humor, and calmness about dangers were massively impressive. He would tell local high school students drawn into the struggle about some of his personal experiences, wanting them to know the dangers they were facing:

He told of his first beating, how they took him out of the cell after dumping the beaten body of his friend back in the cell. He said he was so mad his body sort of became detached and the blows didn't hurt even though they knocked a tooth loose. Mac related this all with a certain easy humor which is the product of being able to look back on terrible experiences. He meets the future with these experiences under his belt. This makes him what the mayor calls a "dangerous rattlesnake." His experience, lack of fear, and easy way of kidding folks into taking risks for the movement make him effective. . . .

Tuesday night four or five houses were pelted with bottles. Last night the small church in which we meet was set on fire. Luckily it isn't far from the house of somebody who is active in the movement. He saw them light it and the fire department arrived to put it out before it did much damage. This morning as we gathered for our staff meeting the sheriff, the mayor, and the FBI arrived. The mayor thought we must have done it since we found out so soon. The FBI didn't even take samples of the broken glass to check for fingerprints. Our main fear now is the haunting question of what is the next step in this escalation.

Yarrow's group went up to Drew, a plantation town to the north, to do the first canvassing the town had experienced. Whites walked through the black neighborhood glaring at the residents. But after a number of canvassing trips to Drew and Indianola, people started signing the freedom forms. A few were willing to go to the courthouse to try to register, like the seventy-year-old man, "with a wooden leg and a strong, piercing gaze." He had been in the First World War and said he hadn't seen more freedom as a result. "He said now he was about to die anyway and would much rather go fighting for freedom than any other way. A few days later he went to the courthouse to try to register and after a long wait was denied."

Yarrow tells how his group was arrested in Drew, Mississippi:

We were holding a rally in a vacant lot with about 15 kids from Drew joining us while the adults watched from across the street. A black student from Mobile, Alabama, gave a song sheet to one of the onlookers. The police arrested him for passing out literature. I was worried about what would happen to Fred so I handed song sheets to some girls on the edge of the rally. A cop rushed across the street and told me to come along. I was taken to a little, square cinder block jail from which I hear Fred's courageous, off-key rendition of a freedom song so I joined him as we came near. Shortly four more of our group joined us. We laughed about how integrated we were, black and white, women and men.

The next evening 30 people were arrested. . . . The little jail was crammed with people and surrounded by grim-faced white men with high-powered rifles in the gun racks of their trucks. The police were nervous. We were bused to the county farm and county jail in Indianola. This time it took several days to raise the $4,800 in bail.

In Indianola the Baptists contributed a school they owned for a freedom school. We had a rally in the new freedom school. The room was packed with 250 people. Over 100 signed up to participate in the freedom school.

The actions of young men and women like Mike Yarrow were only a small beginning, which cost them dearly: Three young civil rights workers were murdered; thirty-seven African-American churches were burned down; eighty volunteers were beaten, and scores were arrested. But the media coverage gave the nation a close look at the violence in Mississippi, and soon the number of blacks registered to vote began to climb.

2 The Ideal or the Practical?

Long after the Freedom Summer, men and women were still acting out the altruism that had prompted their journey to the South. Many had made a lifetime commitment to helping others. One of the college students who went on to law school used his skills to provide legal services for migrant workers. In taped conversations with Robert Coles he said:

> *I never thought I'd end up being a lawyer. . . . Most of us left the South by 1965; the job seemed done so far as we were concerned. We went back to our lives. I finished college, and then took time off again, only it wasn't to do "good," but just to travel and think. I felt I was spoiled rotten to be able to do that, bum around, hitchhike through England and Scotland. In Glasgow I saw the terrible slums, and I was just made sick. The old refrain started again in my head: Why is it that so many people are poor, and mean-*

while others live like fat hogs, wanting more and more, and to hell with everyone else? I tried to get a job in one of the community service centers in a Glasgow slum, and while I was being interviewed I thought to myself this is stupid. Go back home and do what you want to do here back there! So, I did go home.

But when I got back I still wasn't sure what I actually wanted to do. I began to think I was sick in the head. . . . I decided to go see a shrink; then I changed my mind. I applied to law school. Then I almost withdrew my application, because I kept thinking I should go back to Mississippi, and try to do some kind of volunteer work there. You can see, I was in real bad shape! Then, I met someone! She was going to law school, and she was two years younger than I—reminding me of all the time off I'd taken.

That young woman changed his life:

She kept reminding me that I'm me, that there's no point in trying to be someone else—such as one of my classmates who's a lawyer working for Gulf Oil, or another who's working for American Airlines. I began to realize that I didn't want to stop criticizing what I didn't like about my country; I wanted to find a way to help others improve their lives—and that way, I'd be improving my own life.

In his long years of work with young people, Dr. Coles has observed many who lead lives of intense moral awareness. He says:

I have noticed, again and again, that those youths who are openly troubled about their commitment to reform as against their desire to live comfortable, respectable lives, are the ones who seem to last longest as active idealists, though not without substantial mental anguish. Such youths state the obvious about themselves—that they simply cannot or will not shake off a youthful idealism in favor of various "practicalities," various "adjustments to reality," as pressed upon them by parents, friends, former college classmates, new acquaintances. Nor are such young idealists only to be found in the more obvious places—among our migrants, among our Indians. Any number of dedicated idealists straddle the world of commerce and philanthropy, and make constant and personal effort on behalf of poor people.

The actions of the civil rights movement had a powerful effect on the nation. One result was the passage of the Civil Rights Act of 1964. It was the most far-reaching civil rights law since the 1870s. It outlawed racial discrimination in all public accommodations and provided greater federal authority in voting and school matters. It also included an equal opportunity provision that banned discrimination in hiring based on race and other grounds. A year later, Congress passed the Voting Rights Act of 1965. Within three years more than a million blacks in the Deep South had registered to vote. Currently there are many thousands of black elected officials nationwide, including several hundred mayors, many heading the government of our country's biggest cities. In 1994, thirty-seven African-Americans are serving as members of Congress, and four hold Cabinet appointments.

Without question, some blacks have greater opportunities now than in the past. Many have made the most of such opportunities. They function as business executives, college professors, politicians, and in many of the other professions.

But a very large number of African-Americans do not make a good living. The truth is that there is more black poverty now than at any time since the 1960s. A major reason: Long decades of racism have kept an extremely high percentage of African-Americans poor and unskilled. Even when times get better, they are not prepared to take advantage of the openings. Over 40 percent of black people live below the poverty line. They keep sliding back in almost every part of life that counts. The gap between white family incomes and minority family incomes has been widening for many years.

Today in Mississippi, and who knows how many other places, there are still young idealists turning away from moneymaking careers to give their energies, their talents, their devotion, to those in need.

Take Dr. Ronald Myers. In the early 1990s he was working in the town of Tchula, Mississippi, about sixty miles north of Jackson. It has 2,000 people. In the winter when there is no agricultural work to be done, 70 percent of the people are unemployed. How and why did the young black physician choose this place to practice medicine? The answer comes from a reporter for the *New York Times*:

> *There aren't many doctors like Ronald Myers, a jazz-playing, Baptist-preaching family practitioner*

whose dream has always been to practice medicine in the kind of place most other doctors wouldn't even stop for a tank of gas.

But there are plenty of places like Tchula, a forlorn patch of Mississippi Delta poverty where it is hard to find a street that's not rutted, a sign that's not crooked, a paint job that's not peeling or a life that's not perched on the brink of economic ruin.

Dr. Myers's story—how hard it has been for him to get here and how hard it may be for him to stay—provides a dispiriting look at health care in rural America. The situation is worsening because the Government's program to provide doctors for the nation's neediest areas is being dismantled as health-care needs continue to grow.

"Working in Tchula, Miss., is like working in a third world country," said Dr. Myers, who became Tchula's only doctor when he opened a clinic this month in an abandoned restaurant next to an empty liquor store. "The needs are that great. So how is it that here's a well-trained physician who wants to come to an area that's desperately poor, and I can't get any assistance? I can't get a loan. I'll take a tongue depressor if someone will give me one. There's a problem somewhere."

In poor rural areas, particularly in the South, regular medical care is seldom more than a distant dream. In areas like Tchula and nearby Belzoni, where Dr. Myers previously worked, infant mortality rates are three times the national average, most women receive little if any prenatal care and people usually see a doctor only when they have no choice.

. . . Dr. Myers is rare in his profession, a physician who went to a good deal of trouble to practice where no one else would. A 33-year-old Milwaukeean who graduated from the University of Wisconsin Medical School, an accomplished jazz pianist and an ordained Baptist minister, he said coming to the rural South was always his goal in medicine.

"I feel God put this burning desire in my heart to serve in the rural areas of the South where the need is the most," said Dr. Myers, whose new clinic office is decorated with black-history and black-pride posters and mementos from his musical career. "I feel right being here. I feel it's what I was called to do." . . .

Dr. Myers operates full time in Tchula while living in a double-wide trailer in Belzoni. . . . To cobble together his clinic, he has had to rely on makeshift financing, advances from medical suppliers and his own wits. He has no lab equipment and does his own urinalysis under a microscope. . . .

Dr. Myers wonders why the Government does not encourage the doctors it brings to rural areas to stay there by helping them set up practices. But increasingly, the problem is not keeping rural doctors but getting them there in the first place. . . .

Dr. Myers, who is greeted with admiring if slightly puzzled cries of "Hi, Doc," as he walks through Tchula's dilapidated business district, seems unfazed by the economic prospects here. He has already arranged for an ophthalmologist, a surgeon and podiatrist to see patients at his Tchula Family Health Center. He doesn't expect to solve the health prob-

lems of the Mississippi Delta. But he wonders whether the statewide educational initiatives that have been hailed as the salvation of the South will mean much if no one addresses the health-care needs.

"Here you're putting all of this money into educational reforms, and you've got these sick, malnourished kids whose mothers never got any prenatal care," he said. "If they're not healthy, how are they going to be able to learn?"

People like Dr. Myers are concerned with the health of the individual, and of the family. What about the health of the earth itself? Could anything be done to slow down and possibly even stop the poisoning of our planet with chemicals?

3 The Web of Nature

In the fight to save the earth and the future of our species a new generation of activists has sprung up. These youngsters see our planet threatened on all sides. Toxic dumping poisons the soil and water, smog chokes the cities, oil blackens the oceans, defiles the beaches, destroys the wildlife. Dozens of conservation groups enlist volunteers to carry the ecological message to those who wield power in corporate boardrooms and halls of legislatures. They preach the Golden Rule: Treat all life and its habitats as we would treat ourselves.

Teenagers have mustered one of the largest armies of volunteers to push the United States into changing its polluting ways. The nation's biggest youth-run ecological organization is the Student Environmental Action Coalition. It started in 1988, at the University of North Carolina, and now has some 1,500 chapters in high schools and colleges. A recent national conference drew 8,000 students.

The coalition is made up several groups. Take YES—Youth for Environmental Sanity—a troupe of eco-crusaders who crisscross the United States rallying support with a mixture of skits, slides, and songs. By 1992 it had inspired over 100,000 junior and senior high school students to start their own eco-clubs. They get their message across with passion: "Who says we can't save the earth?

Altruism, in its biological sense, is required of us. We have an enormous family to look after, or perhaps that assumes too much, making us sound like official gardeners and zookeepers for the planet, responsibilities for which we are probably not yet grown-up enough. We may need new technical terms for concern, respect, affection, substitutes for altruism. But at least we should acknowledge the family ties and, with them, the obligations. If we do it wrong, scattering pollutants, clouding the atmosphere with too much carbon dioxide, extinguishing the thin carapace of ozone, burning up the forest, dropping the bombs, rampaging at large through nature as though we owned the place, there will be a lot of paying back to do and, at the end, nothing to pay back with.

—Lewis Thomas
research pathologist and author

If we don't save it for ourselves, nobody's going to save it for us!"

When a polling group asked 10,000 young people what their favorite cause was, 75 percent listed the environment as number one. Parents may have grown tired and frustrated after decades of effort, but their children have taken on the fight with fresh ardor. "Reduce, Reuse, Recycle" is their cry as they survey their homes and their communities to see how much trash is produced, how much energy is consumed, and how much water is used.

The young people use every form of pressure they can devise or adapt to get results. Kids Against Pollution (KAP) began in Closter, New Jersey, to protest the use of foam containers in their school cafeteria. Pressuring the board of education, the mayor, and the town council, they got the substance banned. Now KAP has over 1,000 chapters in the United States and abroad, activating kids from grade school through high school.

A tactic that's proved very effective is putting the heat directly on corporate executives whose companies are guilty of pollution. After seeing a documentary film about dolphins being slaughtered in tuna nets, one youngster in Maine got the students in high school biology classes to bombard the top executives at H. J. Heinz Company, the biggest producer of canned tuna, with postcards. A few months later, Heinz announced it would stop buying, processing, or selling tuna caught at the cost of dolphin deaths. KAP members used a similar mailing tactic on McDonald's, urging the company to give up the use of foam containers. Such pressure made the company decide to switch to paper-based wrappings.

News of young people's enthusiasm for environmental protection has its effects elsewhere. Marvel Comics launched *Captain Planet*, a comic book based on the adventures of an international band of youngsters who fight the polluters of the earth. The Small World Products Group introduced Animal Grahams, a line of crackers that depicts eleven endangered species. They are made of organically grown flour and are packaged in biodegradable boxes lettered in soybean ink. A small percentage of the wholesale price goes to environmental causes.

The boycott—a venerable means of pressure—has been mustered by many youth groups to turn corporate polluters away from their harmful practices. One target has been Levi Strauss and Company, for producing acid- and stonewashed jeans. The jeans are made with pumice, a volcanic rock excavated by strip-mining, a process that devastates the landscape. Another corporate target is Mitsubishi, the giant Japanese conglomerate that finances logging in the rain forests of Latin America.

The major adult organizations in the environmental field have multiplied their membership in recent years. The names of these groups are familiar: Sierra Club, National Audubon Society, Environmental Defense Fund, National Wildlife Federation, Wilderness Society, Defenders of Wildlife, to cite only some. But there are many volunteers who labor in grassroots organizations that have learned from the civil rights and women's move-

A team member of the Youth Conservation Corps collects trash along a Pennsylvania highway. *(David Strickler/The Image Works)*

ments of a generation ago. Their philosophy is tagged "biospherical egalitarianism." It simply means that "all things are part of the web of nature," as Alston Chase, an environmental writer, puts it. "The world is not a giant supermarket but a fragile system in which we should play

Greenpeace volunteers confront a Japanese whaler, the *Kyo Maru No. 1*, in Antarctic waters. *(Greenpeace/Culley)*

one small role. All things are equal, and we must not exploit other forms of life. This is a powerful idea whose time has come, convincing key members of a generation that nothing short of complete cultural revolution will save the planet."

Bands of activists use the tactics others developed long ago—letter writing, picketing, lobbying, lawsuits. And they conduct boycotts, sit-ins, and direct actions, like the carefully planned maneuvers of civil disobedience that stem from the principles advanced by Thoreau, Gandhi, and Martin Luther King, Jr.

Members of Greenpeace, for instance, who seek to protect whales and other sea mammals, place themselves in small boats between whaling ships and their prey. Earth First!, another direct-action group, aims to stop construction in wild areas by pulling up survey markers, cutting power lines, and clipping fences. The damage to property, which some call vandalism, they call legitimate nonviolent tactics.

Such people, who act upon their conscience, are sometimes punished severely by governments fearful of criticism. Their fate can be grim, but they do not suffer it alone and forgotten, as we shall see. . . .

4 Prisoners of Conscience

In many parts of the world, there are people who suffer unjustly for their *beliefs*. Seeking to help them, a London lawyer, Peter Benenson, founded Amnesty International (AI) in 1961. It is a worldwide organization concerned exclusively with human rights. Both adult and student volunteers work for the release of people jailed for their beliefs, provided that they have not used or advocated violence. In 1992 AI helped secure the release of 1,041 of these "prisoners of conscience." The actions taken by its volunteer members signify to the world that people do care, and that injustice, torture, mass killings, and mock trials are not just passing news items that are quickly forgotten.

Looking at the record might make anyone cynical about governmental concern for human rights. In recent years tens of thousands of people have been deliberately killed in many parts of the world by government agents acting beyond the limits of the law. They were victims of executions that evaded the judicial process. AI reports of them:

> *Killing grounds were many and varied. Some alleged opponents of governments or people targeted because of their religion, ethnic groups, language or political beliefs were killed in full public view; others in secret cells and remote camps. Some victims were shot down near battlefields, others in mosques and churches, hospital beds, public squares and busy city streets. Prison cells and courtyards, police stations, military barracks and government offices were all sites of political killing by agents of the state. Many people were killed in their own homes, some in front of their families.*
>
> *Victims were assassinated by snipers, blown up by explosive devices or gunned down in groups by assailants using automatic weapons. Others were stabbed, strangled, drowned, hacked to death or poisoned. Many were tortured to death. In Colombia, Guatemala, El Salvador, Syria and the Philippines victims were often severely mutilated before they were killed. Their bodies were burned or slashed, ears and noses were severed and limbs amputated. In many countries prisoners died as a result of torture.*

Methods used included beating, electric shocks, drugs, immersion in water, and hanging. Some persons died as a result of deliberate neglect—by being denied medical attention, by exposure, or from starvation.

Yet as far back as 1948 the world's governments had

committed themselves to the Universal Declaration of Human Rights, a document prepared by the United Nations. A disillusioned observer said, "The only thing universal about human rights is their universal violation." During 1991 serious violations of human rights were reported in 142 countries.

AI estimates that thousands of people are in jail today principally for their beliefs. To persuade governments to set such prisoners free, or at least improve their condition, is AI's task. A staff of researchers at its headquarters in London follows news of arrests, investigates individual cases of prisoners, and monitors governmental repression. When the AI's investigatory standards are met, a case sheet is made up for adoptable prisoners, and that person's case is then assigned to a working group of AI volunteers. The action group bombards the government and prison officials in question with letters urging reconsideration of the case and release of the prisoner. It also writes embassies, leading newspapers, international organizations, organizations related to the prisoner's occupation, and the prisoner's relatives and friends. Whenever possible, the group provides financial aid to the prisoner's family.

Pressure on behalf of a prisoner may go on for months and years, with the AI group using letters, petitions, protests, appeals—whatever measures would seem to help. Almost always a close kinship with the prisoner grows, and sometimes, when their campaign is successful, the group meets the person they've helped set free. There are now some 4,000 local AI groups in sixty-two countries, and more than 700,000 members in over 150 countries.

Student volunteer groups are among Amnesty International's activists in schools and colleges throughout the country. Here Boston volunteers, calling themselves Students for Students, distribute literature and gather signatures at the Government Center, carry picket signs in human rights marches, and *(right, top)* help letter-writers appeal to governments for the freeing of prisoners of conscience. *(Amnesty International U.S.A., Northeast Regional Office)*

Among AI's activists are student volunteer groups in over 600 high schools and colleges across the country. Started by and run by the students, the groups vary in size from a half-dozen members to more than 100. They come together to form a stronger voice against the abuses of human rights. Ten students, alone, may be able to write ten letters for prisoners of conscience, but the same number working together may mobilize hundreds of people to write letters and raise the consciousness of a school to the horrors of human rights violations.

In Massachusetts, the Brockton High School AI group made visible to the whole community their commitment to helping people in trouble by building a "Wall of Human Rights," thirteen feet high, across the school lobby. It was decorated with students' poems, posters, cartoons, expressions of their feelings about freedom struggles in China, Guatemala, South Africa, Vietnam, and even American cities torn by racism and poverty. The group reached out to the school's 4,000 students with the message that freedom can't be taken for granted. Other schools across the United States built human rights walls at the same time.

In rural Pennsylvania the students of Allentown College of St. Francis de Sales, a small Catholic school, formed an AI group several years ago. At first they met with apathy and even hostility from fellow students, but far from being discouraged, they moved ahead with greater determination. Within two years they were recognized as the most active and respected organization on campus. They arranged talks on campus by two former prisoners of conscience from South Africa and Archbishop Denis Hurley, head of the country's Catholic church. They presented two video programs, on the Universal Declaration of Human Rights and on capital punishment, and brought students to a Human Rights Now! concert in Philadelphia. One of the unique methods of making the community aware of human rights issues has been their annual Christmas Luminaria. In remembrance of prisoners of conscience around the world, the campus is lit up with hundreds of candles on the evening of the Christmas dinner. The people on campus sponsor each candle with a contribution to the AI fund.

Each semester the group holds campuswide write-a-thons, which have resulted in the release of at least four prisoners of conscience. Numerous petitions are circulated all year long. The group also developed a campus human rights library, receiving donations of books, audiovisual materials, and funds from many other organizations. As in all other such groups, the members create every imaginable means to awaken and activate the community's concern for human rights.

Of course AI does not work alone. Other organizations, such as the many human rights watch groups, share in the work of curbing violations of human rights wherever they may occur.

When helping efforts on this scale are planned, it takes money—sometimes considerable sums—to carry out the program. Where does the funding come from? Who gives it, and why?

5 A Common Humanity

Money has long been the measure of achievement in American society. We keep score by it. Who's up? Who's down? Who's on top? Our incentive system is built upon financial reward. The purpose of work, if one has to work, seems to be to amass wealth. During the 1980s, the country's one million millionaires grew at the rate of another 100,000 a year.

For those who lack wealth, and that's most of us, money has its attractions. There are few who do not want to live comfortably. Yet there is a trend, visible recently, toward working not for money alone but for something different, something of human, not cash, value. Even some of the young rich are shifting to using their money for nonprofit social ventures.

But before going into why and how this is happening, let's look at philanthropy itself. The dictionary says the word means "love for mankind, devotion to human welfare, goodwill to all." What it calls for are *acts* of goodwill that contribute to people's well-being.

How philanthropic are we? In 1990 Americans gave $122.6 billion to charities. The total rose to $124 billion in 1992. (See box, p. 36.) The largest share of contributions, over half, went to religious groups and institutions. Smaller sums went to education, health care, and the arts and humanities.

Who gave the money? Individuals gave by far the most, with nine of every ten dollars coming from them. Bequests from estates, foundations, and business enterprises were much below that figure.

About 75 percent of all U.S. households donate to charity. They give an average of $790 a year to such causes as education, the environment, health care, homelessness, and the arts. As one commentator said, "Few nations rival the United States in its collective lust to get. But none rival it in its collective urge to give."

> *There is a civil war in our society today, a conflict between two American cultures, each holding very different values. The adversaries are private profits versus public responsibility; personal ambition versus the community good; quantitative measures versus qualitative concerns.*
>
> —Joan Konner
>
> dean, Columbia School of Journalism

Note a curious fact: During the 1980s, while the incomes of the rich rose at a pace unmatched since the 1920s, they gave a far smaller share of their income to charity. It dropped from 7 percent of their after-tax income to less than 4 percent. So although the rich were getting more and more, they were giving less and less. And at the other extreme, the poor were getting less and less, and needing more and more.

It was John D. Rockefeller, together with Andrew Car-

Charitable giving rose to more than $100 billion in 1992. The money came from individuals, corporations, and foundations. As usual, the largest part of it came from individual donors. More money—nearly $57 billion—went to religion than to anything else. Education was next, with $14 billion. Then came human services, $9 billion; health, over $10 billion; and the arts and humanities with about $9 billion. Groups involved with community development, civil rights, and other public activities received $5 billion, while environmental groups got $3 billion. The total sum given for philanthropy was a 6.4 percent increase over the previous year.

Recent studies show, however, that although the income of the rich rose in the 1980s at a pace unprecedented since the 1920s, on the average they gave a smaller share of their income to charity. The new data, supplied by the Treasury Department, showed that wage earners gave a larger percentage of their income to charity than the wealthy. Do the country's top moneymakers grow less altruistic as they grow richer?

negie, the steel magnate, who created the institutional model for American philanthropy. Back in 1913 Rockefeller, using some of his huge fortune from the Standard Oil Company, created the Rockefeller Foundation. Today it is one of the country's ten wealthiest philanthropies, with assets of $2 billion. Its money has financed other great institutions besides the foundation, such as the University of Chicago and Rockefeller University.

Recently the Rockefellers challenged the country's biggest foundations to help alleviate poverty in the third world and to protect the endangered global environment. Peter Goldmark, the Rockefeller Foundation's president, said, "In a period of planetary environmental danger, global communications, intercontinental missiles, a world economy and an international marketplace of ideas and arts and political trends, there is simply no excuse not to."

In 1990, the ten largest American foundations, which had $25 billion in assets, were spending about $100 million for such international programs. One of the world's richest men, Prince Karim Aga Khan, gives away about $130 million a year, much of it to aid schools, medical facilities, and housing in poor African communities.

To offer a helping hand to human beings in distress would seem so natural a thing to do it hardly needs praise as a virtue. But when multimillionaires like Andrew Carnegie and Rockefeller launched their philanthropies the aim was to erase their public image as ruthless industrial barons. Rockefeller piously proclaimed, "I believe the power to make money is a gift of God . . . to be turned to the best of our ability for the good of mankind." That, replied Mr. Dooley, a popular humorist of that period, makes the rich "a kind iv a society f'r th' previntion iv croolty to money." One millionaire of Rockefeller's heyday was blunt about his wealth: "We are the rich," he said, "we own America, we got it, God knows how, but we intend to keep it if we can."

That arrogance was witnessed in two of the most notorious incidents in labor's long struggle to organize. They were the 1892 Homestead steel strike in Pennsylvania and the 1913 Ludlow coal strike in Colorado. Indifferent to the human needs of their employees, companies controlled by Carnegie and Rockefeller brought about the deaths of many workers.

Such bloody disasters horrified the nation. To regain public support, the public relations advisers of the tycoons erected charity by the wealthy into a supreme excellence. What they were trying to do, observed John Dewey, the philosopher and educator, was to make charity

> *an excuse for maintaining law and social arrangements which ought themselves to be changed in the interests of fair play and justice. "Charity" may even be used as a means for administering a sop to one's social conscience while at the same time it buys off the resentment which might otherwise grow up in those who suffer from social injustice. Magnificent philanthropy may be employed to cover up brutal economic exploitation. Gifts to libraries, hospitals, missions, schools may be employed as a means of*

rendering existing institutions more tolerable, and of inducing immunity against social change.

To a degree, the public relations strategy was a success. At the same time, it is true that the philanthropy of the wealthy has done a great amount of good. In 1989 the private foundation of the Coca-Cola Company said it would distribute $50 million during the 1990s to support educational institutions and programs throughout the United States, from elementary schools to universities. At the same time RJR Nabisco announced its foundation would spend $30 million a year to spur minority programs in the schools. General Electric set aside $20 million and IBM $25 million for programs to help education. These commitments were welcomed as examples of "enlightened self-interest," for without a well-educated workforce, American business would be badly handicapped in the competitive world market.

Concerned to better the educational performance of poor children, especially those from minority groups, the Rockefeller Foundation in 1990 said it would spend $15 million in the next five years to build the partnership of teachers, parents, and pupils. The program was developed by Dr. James Comer, a professor of child psychiatry at Yale. He introduced it over twenty years ago in a New Haven public school, and since then it has been adopted in more than seventy schools in nine regions. Under the Comer plan local schools are managed by an active partnership of school staff and students' parents that works to improve students' self-confidence and ultimately their performance.

The many heirs to the Rockefeller dynasty are examples of a younger generation of the rich using their money for a social purpose. There are now twenty-two fourth-generation members of the family. These cousins include physicians, lawyers, educators, and environmentalists. They contribute to the schools where they studied, the communities in which they live, and to a range of very diverse interests: the arts and sciences, health, civil rights causes, and both local and global environmental projects.

In the mid-1980s a group of wealthy young men and women decided it wasn't enough to invest their assets and give away only a small part of their income. They found, after some research, that they weren't alone. Dozens of others had given away assets, ranging from hundreds of thousands to tens of millions of dollars. Strengthened by their discovery, members of the group gave away large parts or nearly all of their wealth. To help others come to the same decision, a few of them collected the personal stories of people who have devoted themselves and their wealth to peace, justice, and the environment.

Their book, *We Gave Away a Fortune*, contains many first-person accounts of how their lives took an altruistic direction. One of them, Chuck Collins, is the great-grandson of Oscar Mayer, founder of a meatpacking fortune. Collins is now director of technical assistance at the Institute for Community Economics (ICE). He helps low-income community groups set up community land trusts and housing cooperatives. And he himself lives in ICE housing on some $8,000 a year. He says:

> *I have great sources of support which give me enough security to let go of my money: good work, community, friends, a support group, and loving relationships. Being part of a larger social movement also increases my sense of security. Perhaps we're only a union of fools trying to build a new society and change our own lives, but I feel inspired and optimistic, knowing that others are doing similar work. Lord knows, I would like to work on behalf of people in Central America, Zaire and the Philippines, but as one person I can do only so much. I feel gratified knowing that I am part of a social movement of people who are doing all this work, and who respect me for doing my piece.*
>
> *We are all utterly interdependent with other human beings. On some deep level we all realize that, but having money can cover it up. So many of us pay someone to grow our food, build our house, pick up our refuse, educate our children. We even have Third World slaves we never meet, mining our fuel and growing our food at ridiculously low wages. I used to buy services and material comforts, which kept me from relying on the spirit, friends, loved ones, my community. But now I am developing a quality of life more connected with others, with less dependence on money. I feel that I have a lot to gain, personally and spiritually, from living more simply; I am learning how to give back my privilege for the long-term*

> *security and sustainability of the earth. Why should I wait for someone else to take the first step in giving up First World privilege?*

A new development is the greater role played by wealthy women in philanthropy. As one of them put it, "We women should use what we have to change the world." In 1981 the Women's Foundation was launched in San Francisco to fund projects of benefit to Bay Area women and girls. It became a bridge between people in need and people with the resources to help them. Since then, other women's funds have been created—nearly fifty by 1990—all serving poor women and girls. Their tendency is to appoint community people to their boards, because who would know better what's needed? As women take greater control of foundation money, the old paternalism is slowly changing. Instead of trying to do *for* people, the funds seek ways to enable them to do for themselves. Such forward-looking leaders see the rich who limit themselves to attending charity balls as self-indulgent, as hungry for publicity on the charity circuit, as not attempting to solve the problem by playing an active role in social change. The newer female philanthropists seek long-term commitments to social needs, rather than brief gestures.

Yet what the rich do is more than matched by what ordinary people do. They give more and volunteer more than the people of any other nation. The facts: As of 1989, 75 percent of all families gave an average of $790 a year to the causes of their choice, 20 million gave 5 percent or more of their income to charity, and 23 million volunteers gave five or more hours a week.

After pointing out with facts and figures the enormous and ever-widening gap between the incomes of rich and poor in the United States, the young philanthropists who wrote *We Gave Away a Fortune*, made this comment:

> *To answer why there are rich and poor in the U.S.—or more precisely, why a small percentage of us have fantastically more wealth than the vast majority—takes sorting through a maze of factors about capitalism: the way money makes money; the way many people's labor is turned into a few people's capital; the way our tax structure benefits the wealthy; the effects of racism and sexism; the impact of the huge military budget on social spending; and so on.*
>
> *Eventually those of us who gave principal sorted out our personal understandings of these issues and resolved that the differences between rich and poor in this country were not justifiable—nor inevitable, nor tolerable. Perhaps our grandfathers who started factories were brilliant and bold, but they still didn't deserve to end up with 100,000 times more money than their employees. And when our $500,000 in stocks brings us a return of $50,000 a year without lifting a finger, while millions of hardworking families work a whole year to earn far less (often finding themselves deeper in debt)—that's not fairness, that's a painfully skewed economic system.*

Where does all this generous activity come from? "The truth is," said Brian O'Connell, a professional in the field, "we don't know. Most likely our generosity comes from a combination of religious ethics, a determination by those who fled oppression to never again be controlled by central government, the freedoms of speech and assembly and the exhilarating experience of being able to band together for influence and to create alternatives."

Several popular notions about generosity don't hold up, according to a study made by O'Connell's group, Independent Sector:

- It isn't the generosity of America's rich that is responsible for the high standard of giving. The not-rich—the middle and working classes—lead the way. Even people who make under $10,000 give 2.8 percent of what they have. Generally, the higher up the economic ladder you go, the smaller the percentage of income given.
- Americans were not more generous with their money and their volunteered time in earlier days. A much bigger part of the population now gives money and volunteers time.
- People in big cities do care. Mutual aid groups are just as common in the cities as in the towns. Almost every problem or crisis finds groups of people who have weathered that storm reaching out to help those facing depression, substance abuse, rape, divorce, death of a spouse or child, and so on.

- It isn't the foundations and big corporations that are the most generous. Important as their help is, they give only 10 percent of all that's contributed. The other 90 percent comes from individuals.
- Tax policies making it easier to donate to charity are not responsible for a large part of the generosity. Giving existed long before there was an income tax, and despite a recent more restrictive tax policy, it goes on rising. The sense of community and compassion is not crippled by tax laws.
- It isn't true that the great increase in women now working for pay makes it harder to get them to volunteer. Such women are more likely to volunteer than the others.

6 No Greater Love

How far back does the generous act of giving of oneself, of caring for others, go?

People have always shared with one another (just as they have always destroyed one another). In the family, tribe, or clan they had to cooperate simply to survive in hostile environments or in defense against hostile strangers. They did it as individuals or in groups.

Historians examining this aspect of our past see two different approaches to the problem of meeting human needs. One is individual service, and the other is social reform. Both the ancient Greeks and the Romans turned to social reform as the way to help poorer citizens and to lighten their burden. The Jewish tradition stressed the duty of kindness to others in need. In Micah's words, "What doth the Lord require of thee, but to do justice and to have mercy and to walk humbly with thy God." And Moses said, "At the end of every three years you shall bring forth all the tithe of your produce in the same year, and lay it within your towns; and the Levite, because he has no portion or influence with you, and the sojourner, the fatherless, and the widow, who are within your towns, shall come and eat and be filled."

Christianity had its roots in Judaism, and its long tradition of help. Jesus said, "This is my commandment, that you love one another as I have loved you. Greater love than this no one has, that one lay down his life for his friends." The early Christian communities tried to provide help to the poor and the sick. For long centuries, however, little was done by the people in power for the poor, the victims of plagues, the mentally ill. It was a struggle to remind people of their common humanity, of their duty to share with another, to love as Christ had loved. Only with the work of St. Francis of Assisi around the year 1200 did lay movements arise to help the poor, the sick, and the old.

Throughout medieval history there was little attention to social reform. Charity meant charity to the individual. During the Reformation, however, parishes in Europe began to form "common chests" for distribution of food, clothing, and money to the needy. In France the Daughters of Charity were formed by St. Vincent de Paul to devote themselves to charitable work, especially the nursing of the poor. These were the forerunners of the modern social worker.

Elizabethan England in 1601 adopted a Poor Law, which recognized that government has a responsibility for the needy. It placed their care in the hands of the local community, the parish. Modified over time, this approach lasted well into the nineteenth century. With the Industrial Revolution various social reform movements succeeded after hard battles in getting laws passed to make more humane the conditions for the disadvantaged. Other European nations and the United States followed that example. Governments gradually played a larger role in problems of health, social welfare, education, housing, and working conditions. None were eager to do so, but eventually they recognized that only government could do for many citizens what they could not do for themselves.

These developments did not come about miraculously. It was volunteers who first saw the needs and devised various means to meet them. By working alone or in association with others they pressed for legislative reforms that would never have been enacted in and of themselves.

In the United States, scant attention was paid to those in need throughout the colonial period. The early pious settlers crossed the ocean with a strong belief in the depravity of the unfortunate. This vast new land, they believed, was a splendid place to make good. If an American failed to grab his share of private property, it was his own fault.

So the poor were despised and degraded, and often treated cruelly. As the small settlements grew into towns and cities, however, a sense of civic pride grew slowly, too. And with it, a concern for one's fellow citizens. Benjamin Franklin was the great pioneer. "Improve yourself," he said, but making the most of your abilities can't be

Benjamin Franklin *(at right)* lending books in the free library he organized in Philadelphia in 1731. It was one of his many voluntary contributions to the betterment of community life. *(The Granger Collection)*

done in isolation. We are social creatures, and we live and grow within a community, to which and for which we are responsible. We help ourselves by helping others. We show our gratitude to God best by "promoting the happiness of his other children."

To Benjamin Franklin, Pennsylvanians—and all of us—owe the establishment of a free library, a hospital, an academy, a university, a volunteer fire department, a police force, schools for African-Americans and Native Americans, and better education for women. He became rich by his own efforts, but he was not a greedy man; business in and of itself gave him no joy. It was only a means to carry out his other goals. Wealth to him meant freedom to be useful to the community.

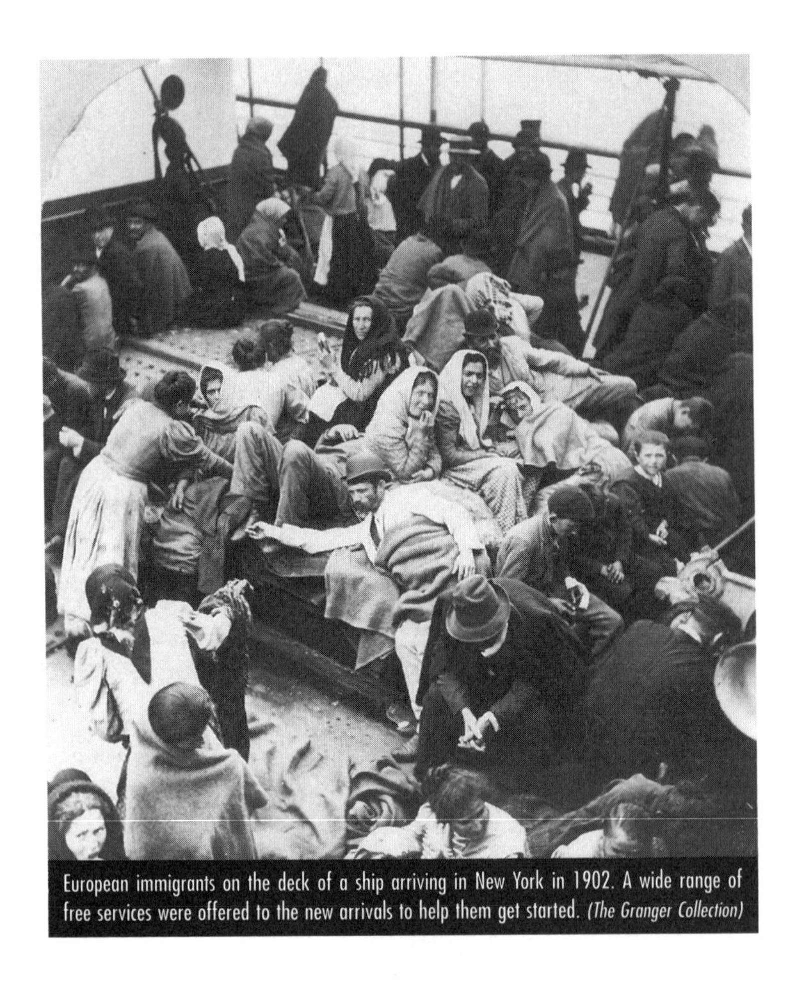

European immigrants on the deck of a ship arriving in New York in 1902. A wide range of free services were offered to the new arrivals to help them get started. *(The Granger Collection)*

But when wave after wave of immigrants began to arrive, starting in the 1840s, they needed more than the generosity of individuals here and there. They needed help to establish themselves in this strange new world. The early settlement houses offered them a unique service while they awakened in the well-to-do the impulse to help the new arrivals. The Jewish community especially took the lead in voluntary effort. It pioneered a wide range of services for the needy immigrants—language classes, job training, clinics, hospitals, relief societies, homes for orphans and the aged. The same era saw the creation of YMCAs, prison reform groups, and schools for the blind and the deaf and the mentally handicapped.

In the twentieth century the voluntary groups grew at an explosive rate. Every imaginable kind sprang up to serve local, regional, and national needs. To give but one example: By the 1970s there were at least seventy-five national voluntary agencies concentrating on a specific disease or medical problem. But voluntary associations alone could not cope with the needs of the poor and the unemployed when the Great Depression of the 1930s crippled the nation. The federal government had to step in and relieve mass economic distress. In 1935 the first permanent Social Security legislation was passed, and amendments in the years since have extended coverage while Medicare has offered the increasing percentage of older persons a stronger sense of security.

In the 1960s, when so many Americans were enjoying prosperity, the country was shocked by the revelations of one man's book. Michael Harrington, in *The Other America*, told the nation what it had tried to ignore: that many millions of Americans lived in poverty. No longer able to turn their backs upon the needy, Congress launched an antipoverty program with many innovative features. It reached down into the local neighborhoods for ideas and help in solving some of the persistent problems that had damaged the lives of masses of Americans over the generations. Both governmental and private agency funds supported the programs. That they were not more successful is due to a number of complex reasons. Blame it on political opportunism and on petty corruption. But more important, too many Americans failed to see beyond this year's tax returns to the long-range benefits the reduction or elimination of poverty would bring to us all. Later, in the 1980s, during the Reagan and Bush administrations, federal aid was cut drastically, and many programs were weakened or scrapped. As cities and states teetered on the edge of bankruptcy, Washington told them, "Go take care of the needy yourselves." They are trying.

In the White House and many other high offices of government and business, something had happened to the concept of love they neighbor as thyself. It had soured into the morality of "me and mine." Behind the

Is it possible that we can produce, if not so much through politics, then through our families, our churches, our schools, with assistance from our media—is it possible that we can see the emergence of Altruistic Man? The instinct for it is there among us. There is a thread of goodness running through the American society. There is a chance that it can be woven into a fabric.

—Eric Sevareid
author and former CBS-TV correspondent

patriotism of flag waving and the talk about "a kinder, gentler" government was a narrow individualism. Sacrifice for others and for causes larger than self-aggrandisement was only for freaks and outcasts, not for leaders. Members of the in-group had value, but in a showdown, the in-group consisted of "me." In such a moral atmosphere Wall Street insider scandals, corruption in Pentagon contracting, criminal pollution by industry, and conflict-of-interest appointments in government were no surprise.

Still, the idea of a common humanity, of concern for others, has not diminished or disappeared. You can still find the desire to help among people in office, whether high or low, whether elected or appointed. Their concern for others, expressed in word or deed, needs encouragement from the rest of us, the Americans who do not hold the reins of power. We should not hesitate to say we expect people in high places to give of themselves in service to others.

7 Hurricanes and Earthquakes

Nineteen ninety-two was the year of Hurricane Andrew. It was a natural, not a man-made, catastrophe. It was the most destructive hurricane in history: winds of 175 miles per hour, billions of dollars in property damage, and scores of thousands of people left homeless.

Three years earlier, in 1989, the United States was hit by Hurricane Hugo, second only to Andrew in devastation. Enough time has passed since Hugo to assess the human response to that crisis.

As soon as Hugo hit, millions of dollars in donations began pouring in to the Disaster Relief Fund of the American Red Cross. Thanks to the overwhelming support of the American people, the agency was able to shelter and feed 129,000 people. This proved, as someone said, "that there is one thing more powerful than Mother Nature: human nature."

The storm brought "both economic deprivation and astonishing generosity," reported a *New York Times* correspondent. As one of the nation's poorest states, South Carolina suffered terribly. "It is always the poor who get hurt the most," said the mayor of Charleston. In his city the poor people "live closest to the economic edge. Their houses are less solid. Their insurance is less extensive. Their jobs are less secure. Their churches have fewer resources."

One of the Carolina communities hardest hit by the storm was McClellanville, a seaside town. If not for the vast volunteer effort from around the country, it would not have been able to survive. A crew of forty-five striking miners from West Virginia showed up unannounced, pitched their tents, and helped the town dig out from the massive debris. Contractors donated building materials, and from the people of Ocean County, New Jersey, came thirty-seven truckloads of food and clothing, three fire trucks and a dump truck, plus electricians and other workers to help the town restore services.

Not far off, in Centerville, nearly every building was badly damaged. A group of volunteers in the Mennonite Disaster Service came in from several states to repair buildings. They would work at it regularly for the next several months. "Without the volunteers, without the one-to-one help," said one Carolinian, "I don't know where we would be. They have been absolutely beautiful." In Charleston, residents not hit by the storm donated $1.1 million to repair the homes of others.

Young people were perhaps the most visible and active

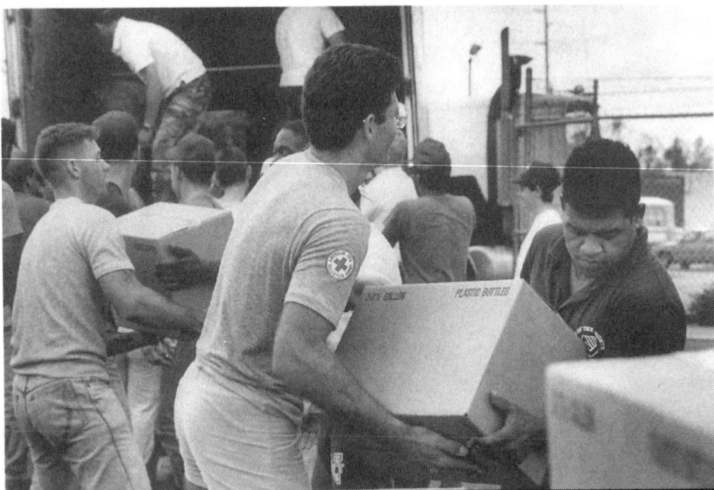

Volunteers for the American Red Cross help victims of the natural disasters that ravage communities and regions: *(top)* A nurse aids a child during the California earthquake of 1989. In the aftermath of Hurricane Hugo in South Carolina, volunteers bring in medical supplies *(bottom)*, take care of children made homeless *(right, top)*, and help the aged and handicapped *(right, bottom)*. *(American Red Cross)*

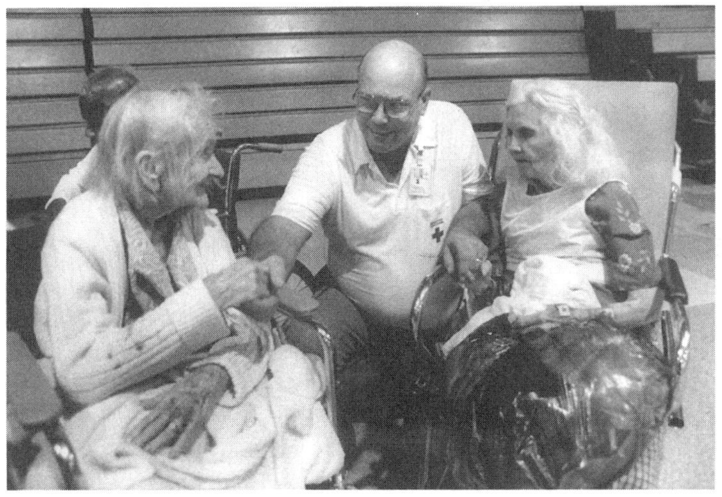

relief workers, including many who were displaced from their own homes at the time. In Charleston, thirteen high school students volunteered at "telephone central" in City Hall taking phone calls from all over the country regarding information and donations, and local calls from people in need. Other boys and girls cleaned up their schools and the yards of elderly and handicapped people unable to do it themselves. They cooked meals for neighbors whose stoves were ruined; did emergency roofing and repairs to damaged houses; sorted donated clothes, food, and supplies and distributed them to people in emergency shelters. From as far off as Pennsylvania, Maryland, and Georgia, young people came in to help.

Many of the Hurricane Hugo volunteers were connected to Youth Service America. Founded in 1986, the nonprofit YSA leads a national movement of grassroots organizers and organizations. Its existence signifies a renewed spirit of involvement in public service by dedicated young Americans. More than 2,000 YSA members rode in or flew in from as far away as New York City to assist with emergency aid and then with clean-up efforts.

While rescue efforts were still focused on the southeastern coast, an earthquake struck northern California. It was nowhere near as devastating as the great quake and fire that destroyed much of San Francisco in 1906. But good Samaritans and volunteers flooded in from miles around. Large numbers of donors rushed to blood banks. People brought food and clothing to the shelters set up by the city. Engineers and building inspectors beyond the stricken area phoned in offers to help. Private water companies sent in drinking water. Men and women with special disaster expertise found their way to the places that needed them.

On the Bay Bridge, which had collapsed in the terrible moments of the quake, volunteers at great risk to their own safety struggled furiously to rescue people trapped in cars or trucks by massive slabs of fallen concrete. When the upper and lower levels of Interstate 880 collapsed after the support columns fell away during the quake, a motorist's car was nearly flattened. But about eighteen inches of space remained between the two highway sections, allowing the man to survive. For two hours a construction worker, Rick Stover, maneuvered painstakingly to get the man out. There proved to be just enough room to pull his hips through. He didn't have a scratch.

Help is not always distributed fairly in disasters. The quake in northern California hit both well-to-do homeowners in the Marina district along the bay and poor people living in welfare lodgings. Both groups were driven out in the streets. But aid to the victims was not so evenhanded, said advocates for the city's poor. The most expensive hotels offered free rooms to quake victims but specified Marina residents only. Only one of these hotels was willing to take anyone who needed a room.

Such inequities were attributed to the inexperience of Red Cross volunteers, most of whom were white and middle-class. They were unprepared for low-income quake victims with drug or alcohol problems or who showed signs of mental illness. About 3,500 poor people left homeless by the quake were now added to the 12,000 who were homeless before the quake. The Red Cross, which raises emergency funds to meet disasters, relies on volunteers and maintains shelter operations only for the first few weeks following a disaster. That is the extent of their responsibility. They cannot remain on the scene indefinitely. It is up to other sources—city, state, federal—to handle the long-range needs.

In San Francisco, some advocates for the homeless said the Red Cross was being unfairly saddled with the problems of the homeless because of the general public's lack of willingness to help.

The Red Cross has a long history of helping others. It is part of an international humanitarian movement that began in the mid-nineteenth century when wars devastated Europe. The American wing is one of the 145 national Red Cross societies, headquartered in Geneva, Switzerland. Since 1881, Americans have turned to the Red Cross for emergency services. Today 1.4 million trained volunteers (135,000 of them young people under the age of eighteen) help their neighbors across the country every day. They assist victims of natural and man-made calamities. The volunteers gather at the scene of more than 40,000 disasters a year, from house fires to devastating floods, tornadoes, and earthquakes.

Early in this century the Red Cross began to recruit thousands of nurses for a public health nursing program to bring better health and hygiene to needy people in rural America. Red Cross instructors trained neighbors in first aid, nursing skills, and water safety. In times of depression or drought, Red Cross workers have distributed millions of bushels of wheat and flour donated by the government. It was the Red Cross that began the recruiting of blood donors and opened the first blood center in hospitals. By the time of World War II there was in nearly every family someone who had either served as a Red Cross volunteer, contributed money or blood, or received Red Cross services.

Red Cross volunteers come from many different backgrounds and have all kinds of skills. They work in health clinics, child-care centers, and hospitals. They collect and distribute blood, drive Red Cross vehicles, visit the elderly, and teach community service courses in health maintenance and accident prevention. They offer to do whatever the community needs.

It all started with Jean-Henri Dunant, a young Swiss businessman. When the Austrians and French were fighting in 1859 he was on the battlefield of Solferino where 40,000 soldiers were killed or wounded and left without help. The kind of man who couldn't stand by doing nothing while others suffered, he had the courage to act on his concern. He started the first Red Cross group. It was his ideas that led to the Geneva Conventions, international treaties designed to protect the victims of all armed conflict.

Dunant is an example of what altruism means. His actions were motivated by the need to feel connected to others. "Community," as Dorothy Day, the founder of the Catholic Worker Movement, said, "is all of us together, trying to help each other." With a kind of mystical faith she once told Robert Coles:

> *We are communities in time and in a place, I know, but we are communities in faith as well—and sometimes time can stop shadowing us. Our lives are*

touched by those who lived centuries ago, and we hope that our lives will mean something to people who won't be alive until centuries from now. It's a great "chain of being," someone once told me, and I think our job is to do the best we can to hold up our small segment of the chain . . . to keep that chain connected, unbroken.

8 Keeping the Chain Connected

Volunteers are all part of the chain of which Dorothy Day spoke. Their numbers are far greater than most of us imagine—over 100 million, by one estimate. A directory listing volunteer opportunities describes more than 5,500 American volunteer groups, although some experts maintain there are actually a hundred times that many. The book guides readers through a full range of national and local volunteer resources programs and training events. Added to the traditional groups are the newer ones directed at combating AIDS, the problems of the homeless, teenage pregnancy, illiteracy, and drug abuse. A recent study reveals that about four out of ten Americans age forty-five and over do volunteer work, and a third of those who don't said they would in the future. A Gallup Poll at the same time found that 41 percent of all Americans do volunteer work.

But who knows about their deeds? Some names—of public officials, corporate executives, sports and entertainment stars—appear time and again in the newspapers. But that is not the case with the names of others whose contributions are no less significant. This is why the *Pittsburgh Post Gazette* publishes regularly feature stories on community people whose friends or neighbors have called their volunteerism to public attention.

Take Richard Romano of Pittsburgh. Some thirty years ago he started the Bloomfield Youth Athletic Association. It began with four baseball teams and by 1990 had twenty-four teams and 450 players. They are divided by age, from kids four to six up through boys fifteen to seventeen. The league plays three games on weeknights and five on Saturday during the summer. Romano is there for nearly every game. He leaves work at the county District Attorney's office at 5:00 P.M. and a few minutes later is at Dean Field, where the kids play until lights out at 11:30. Romano had a heart attack when he was thirty-six and has been hospitalized seven times since then. "I think God gave me twenty-some years to keep going," he said. "If it weren't for these kids I might have died. It keeps me young."

When Herman Mitchell was a child, he used to recite poetry to the ladies at the Lemington Home for the Aged, where his mother was a longtime volunteer. Many years later, when the home was threatened with financial collapse, Police Commander Mitchell organized a massive grassroots campaign in the black churches that generated more than $50,000 in small pledges. The amount was enough to convince local foundations, corporations, and government that Lemington was vital to the community. With a $2.5-million endowment goal approaching fulfillment, the home was assured its commitment to poor elderly people with no place else to go would be honored.

Charlotte Cohen is a grandmother in her seventies with thirty years of experience volunteering. Hers is a passionate concern for the underprivileged. She's looked at the big picture, identified key needs, and plugged herself into many organizations to bring about major changes. In her city of Pittsburgh she played a vital role in getting a housing maintenance code adopted. She secured the future of a centralized city rehabilitation agency. She got the government to fulfill a promise to replace wartime housing. Her efforts brought about a citywide rodent control program and a system of emergency repair service to assist those too frail or poor to cope with a broken furnace, damaged roof, or other unexpected costly mishaps.

A missionary couple, Dan and Kathy Blackburn, went to Haiti in 1976 with their two sons and started a ministry in a small mountain village. Soon they were taking care of sick or abandoned children, bringing them under their roof. When the Duvalier government collapsed, the Blackburns and the children had to flee to the Dominican Republic because the rebels threatened to kill them. Late in 1989 they returned to their home state of Indiana with twenty-eight Haitian children—ranging in age from one year to fourteen—whose natural parents are dead, unknown, or untraceable. Admitted under humanitarian parole, the children were adopted by the Blackburns.

A thirteen-year-old named Justin Lebo builds bicycles for other boys who can't afford them. In 1987 Justin began buying, begging, or scrounging from trash cans hundreds of bikes, most no more than hulks, and rebuilding them into usable bikes for children in nearby towns of New Jersey. Justin lives in the working-class community of Saddle Brook and has always loved bikes. He bagan racing them on a dirt track at the age of eight. At ten he took his first junked bike and rebuilt it into a "Super Bike." His father, Michael, stripped the frame to bare metal and sprayed it with shiny black lacquer; his mother, Diane, painted in the silver striping. Justin went on to rebuild two more bikes, then asked Diane to find a children's home that needed bikes. Within two years the twenty-nine boys at Kilbarchan, a home for children in need, each had his own bike, thanks to Justin.

Justin says he did it because he knows how he'd feel if he didn't have a bike. And he likes to fix bikes. "It's really no big deal."

But to the boys at the home it is. "These kids feel the world has kicked them out," says one of the staff. "Justin wasn't some rich kid who went out and bought brand new bikes with his big allowance. This was a kid who cared enough to give up things so he could help these kids."

Sometimes volunteering starts with an intensely personal experience. June Bingham, a writer, sat by the bedside of her husband, Jonathan, a former congressman,

June Bingham, who established the Trained Liaison Comforters at Columbia Presbyterian Medical Center in New York. *(J. Bingham)*

every day while he lay dying in an intensive care unit of the Columbia Presbyterian Medical Center in New York. She noticed how alone many other gravely ill patients were. For whatever reason, there was no one at their bedside.

Now at the medical center there is a corps of volunteers, established by Mrs. Bingham, known as the Trained Liaison Comforters or TLCs. They explain medical procedures, run errands, offer a sympathetic ear, and comfort the family and friends of the critically ill. Their mission is to offer the "tender loving care" that the group's initials suggest.

The project brings together a social worker, an educational program, and trained volunteers to provide comfort and emotional support. The volunteers each work a four-hour shift daily during visiting periods. While the hospital staff takes care of the patient's medical needs, the TLCs concentrate on helping the family and friends of the patient.

Older New Yorkers trying to live more active and therefore healthier lives are being helped by a legion of volunteers trained to keep them fit. Stay Well is the city's program, and it relies on volunteers who must be at least sixty years old themselves. The program reaches 3,500 people weekly, mainly at some eighty centers for the elderly throughout the city. There are about 1.3 million New Yorkers over the age of sixty, so the program has a long way to go. But it sets a model that proves such a program can work, and other cities are beginning to copy it.

Even great-grandmothers in their eighties are leading classes. They serve as an inspiring model for other seniors who feel, "If she can do it, I can do it." Over 400 instructors have gone through the twelve-week training session and six-week follow-up course. The instructors focus on centers in low-income neighborhoods where people are harder to reach than people living in middle-class areas.

Many churches have extensive outreach programs that rely on volunteers. At the Cathedral Church of St. John the Divine in New York, a community of care has been built up. The volunteers teach the young; visit homebound seniors; shelter the homeless; feed the hungry; care for children after school; and help teenagers get off drugs, stay in school, and train for work.

Isaac Quinerly, for instance, is a volunteer and former client at the Cathedral Kitchen and the Shelter. He is currently working for a security company while studying to renew his license as a paramedic. Returning to New York from Chicago, where his father and sister had just died, he needed help, he recalls, and came to the Cathedral Shelter:

> *I knew there was a shelter here. I came in here on a Wednesday, and my bed was ready for me on Thursday. What was most important coming into this program with no money was that they provided me with dollars for transportation; they provided me with two meals a day, clean sheets, clean towels, soap, shaving gear, brushes, a clean place to sleep. You cannot go out and look for a job dirty. You need to be presentable and clean, and smelling like a human being. All*

I needed was to get out on the streets and beat the pavement to get what I wanted.

I got a letter from Canon Pridemore, and the director of Adult Education at Borough Manhattan Community College accepted it. I was given a $350 grant to renew my license as a paramedic. The $40 I needed for books I paid myself.

If you don't have people like Canon Pridemore or the Cathedral to fall back on, you're really a number. The system feels that they have people asking for public aid who have a tendency to make a career out of this. That's not true. I have a purpose here, to do what I know best.

The tack I'm taking in this place is immense, but I love the community part of it. Being willing to put something back in is important. Nobody asked me to give $10 towards these guys' carfare, but I'm working now. I can help them. I feel I can help somebody.

As a youngster, Frankie Thomas got into trouble early on. When interviewed, he was in the Cathedral's Manhattan Valley Youth Outreach. After nine months in its Transformations program, he got a job in the Cathedral Shop as a maintenance man:

I came here from jail. Actually, I got probation, and my group home sent me. I was 16, playing with this gun with my friends, and the cops came. They all ran away, and I got caught holding it.

It was nothing new. I'd been in and out of j.d. places. At school, anywhere, I was always fighting. Nothing else. Just fighting.

I liked the Valley right away. They didn't let any-

body stay around if they were gonna be failures. Discipline. That's what I wanted, that's what I needed. They want you to have a sense of order. They were straight. They never disrespected me. They told me the truth and I listened.

Mainly, I had a bad temper. They showed me how to control it. There's a lot of love down there in the Valley. They tell you how your future will be if you do those things. And I didn't want it to be those things.

I was on the Lead Team. We cleaned parks, schools, and we silk-screened T-shirts. I loved that. I cut half of the designs for the shirts we made over the summer. I'm doing this job at the Cathedral Shop now, because that's where I have experience. But I just took my GED test for the second time. Waiting for the results. We'll see then, maybe I'll take some classes. I want to be successful.

At the Valley they give you support. Get you going. Now I want to be able to tell the truth; that I was in prison. Now I have friends, people you can be truthful with.

9 The Poor Ones, the Broken Ones

A society must be judged by how it cares for those who are weakest.

Plato, the Greek philosopher, said that about the elderly 2,500 years ago.

Today it's still the elderly, but added to them are the homeless, the victims of AIDS, the unemployed, the illiterate, and all the others who have no share in the affluence enjoyed by the top crust of society.

Let's start with the homeless. In 1994, in New York City alone, authorities estimated there were about 100,000 homeless people. They were seen everywhere—in the subways and alleys, on the streets and park benches, and in doorways. But an innovative new program launched by Volunteers of America (VOA) was bringing a glimmer of hope to the desperate needy. Called Operation Outreach, it is designed to reach the most fragile homeless groups—women, children, people

To illustrate the variety of opportunities open to volunteers, here is a list taken from one issue of the *Boston Globe*. Almost any community could provide the same kinds of openings. Look about you, and you'll see what you could do.

VOLUNTEER OPPORTUNITIES

Boston Community Services. Is seeking volunteers to become members of its Human Rights Committee. Members will advocate the rights of people with mental illness and meet once a month. Lawyers, paralegals and individuals with a human service background are needed for the committee.

Newton-Wellesley Hospital. Volunteers needed to deliver Sunday newspapers to patients in the hospital.

Milton Hospital. Seeks volunteers to work in gift shop and at transportation desk.

New England Aquarium. Whale watch volunteers needed. Become a marine interpreter and educate passengers on board the *Voyager II* about whales, whale ecology and conservation, and habitat protection. Volunteers are asked to donate a minimum of three hours per week, days and weekends, and must be at least 16 years of age.

La Alianza Hispana. Tutors needed to work with Spanish adults studying English and who are also preparing for their GED exam.

Halcyon Place. Volunteers needed to serve as receptionists, hosts, and to perform office duties.

Norfolk Mental Health Association. Volunteers needed to distribute literature, plan the auction, and help market the "Spring Fling" event.

Computer Museum. Volunteers needed to assist in all phases of publicity and promotion and other operations of the Public Relations department.

Masspirg. Volunteers needed for various administrative tasks. Minimum of 3 hours a week and a three-month commitment.

Shortstop Inc. An emergency shelter for homeless adolescents is gearing up for its annual fund drive. Volunteers needed to answer phones, do light typing, mailing, and other administrative duties. Hours and days are extremely flexible.

American Cancer Society. Volunteer drivers are needed to bring cancer patients to and from treatment appointments through the Society's Road to Recovery program. Appointments take place weekdays during business hours. A car and safe driving skills are needed. Free training provided; flexible schedule.

Massachusetts Coalition for a Healthy Future. Collect signatures on a petition to help reduce smoking among children, sponsored by the American Cancer Society and more than 25 other organizations. Signature collection takes place May 6 through June 17. Volunteers are also needed to distribute literature and work in the campaign office.

Outdoor Explorations. Volunteers needed for outdoor cleanup/fund-raiser event April–July for people with and without disabilities. Free T-shirt to first 100 registrants. One- to three-day involvement.

A Volunteers of America team reaches out to homeless men near the World Trade Center in New York with offers of food, clothing, and shelter. *(Antonio Mari for VOA)*

with AIDS, and those so weakened by malnourishment, disease, and hopelessness that their lives are in danger on the streets.

The volunteers go into the public places where homeless people congregate for warmth and security. They enter bus terminals, subway tunnels, and the lower reaches of other buildings to bring food, water, on-site emergency medical care, and other immediate services. Wherever they go, they try to build the trust needed to bring the homeless into shelters, where they can get counseling, substance-abuse treatment, and other services that will help them make a better life for themselves.

The results are very promising. About 80 percent of the homeless who are reached by the program—more than 600 per month—succeeded in finding a better place to live. VOA itself now operates New York's largest shelter for homeless men, under the auspices of the city's Human Resources Administration.

On the West Side of Manhattan, there is a Catholic school whose cafeteria is used as a shelter for fifteen homeless women. Each evening, volunteers convert it into a dormitory. When the call went out for physically fit people to set up beds before the women came, neighbors responded. The volunteers have to fold and put away cafeteria tables, sweep the floor, put up heavy metal collapsible beds with mattresses, and bring out sacks of clean sheets and towels. Two volunteers each night stay in to oversee the dormitory, sleeping on cots. At 6:30 A.M. other volunteers arrive to reverse the routine, lugging the beds back into closets. It's a hard job, reports one young woman volunteer. She says, "There is nothing noble about it. It just soothes my conscience. I work in the Pan Am building, and I must step over a dozen of these people every day between home and work. It makes you think."

In Chicago, volunteers gave their weekends to fixing up abandoned apartments in a rundown public housing project. At first they were only a dozen parishioners from middle-class and mostly white churches. Their example led tenants themselves in the Cabrini-Green complex to repaint walls that hadn't been touched for decades. The effort proved so effective that soon 70 to 100 volunteers each weekend, joined by tenants, were reclaiming dozens of apartments rendered unlivable by gangs, vandals, drug dealers, and squatters. "This is the very essence of community," according to one volunteer.

Cabrini's bleak buildings house more then 10,000 people, most on some sort of welfare. The volunteers appeared weekends at 8:15 A.M., put on hard hats, and spread out through the housing project. Some groups cleaned, some painted, some installed floor tiles, some scoured dirt and grease off walls and cabinets during the eight-hour shifts.

The program moved the local housing authority to expand the volunteer effort to public housing elsewhere in Chicago. The idea of volunteer labor in such projects became part of a larger strategy to improve the lives of tenants. It boosted the morale of the tenants, showing that there are people who really do care. It made them feel they are not alone.

Feeding the hungry is another vital need that volunteers try to meet. Just ten years ago there were only a

College student volunteers clean up a low-income neighborhood in Austin, Texas. *(B. Daemmrich/The Image Works)*

handful of soup kitchens in New York. In 1992 there were more than 700 food programs—the soup kitchens that serve hot meals, and food pantries that supply carry-out food packages. They provide 2.5 million meals each month. To illustate how rapidly the number of hungry people has grown, one soup kitchen served some 50,000 meals in 1989. In 1991, it served nearly twice as many. Not only do the volunteers provide meals, but they help clients fight evictions, get drug treatment, and apply for food stamps. And of course they are constantly on the hunt for funds to run their programs.

There are some professions whose very nature implies an obligation to help others. Medicine is one of the most obvious. The function of the physician is to take care of and heal the sick. All doctors do this in the course of their everyday work, and most are very well paid for it. But some, like Dr. Andrea Fox, go beyond routine care.

In her thirties, Dr. Fox makes house calls to sick elderly people who cannot leave their homes. For most doctors the elderly are not a priority. Dr. Fox was raised to see things differently. Her grandmother organized New York's garment workers, and as a child Andrea was taken on many peace marches. She grew up with a social conscience. She took her residency at the Montefiore Medical Center in the Bronx partly because it has a program focused on the health needs of the poor. Dr. Fox specialized in geriatrics and started a program called the Physician Visits for the Homebound Elderly, into which she drew other doctors and nurses. Supported by several foundations, it serves the people of the Bronx. It isn't easy work that makes you rich, but with an aging population it becomes a more vital service every day.

Dr. Neil Kahanovitz is another example of a physician who stretches himself beyond the routine. When the terrible earthquake shook Armenia in 1988, the orthopedic surgeon volunteered to operate on quake victims. He made five trips to the region to care for people desperate for his skills. The Soviet Union gave him an award for his "courageous and selfless actions."

The health problems of the nation's homeless are staggering. They struggle for survival every day and don't seek health care until they're badly hurting. This means minor illnesses turn into serious and costly medical problems. Studies by medical teams show these problems include very high rates of serious respiratory conditions, such as pneumonia and tuberculosis, and a variety of foot problems, including poor circulation and infections. In some shelters about 30 percent of the homeless are infected with the AIDS virus. Homeless families with children (one of every four homeless people is a child) are a major challenge. The children get no well-child care, such as screening for sickle cell anemia and routine immunizations for diseases like polio and measles.

About 100 homeless health-care programs were operating in 1990, receiving some federal money for the treatment of more than 20,000 patients. Foundations supported some medical projects for the homeless, especially those doing experimental work. But most health care for the homeless relies heavily on charity and volunteers. Louisville, Kentucky, provides an example of the medical profession's willingness to help. When the Jefferson County Medical Society took over a 200-bed men's shelter, many of its members offered free health care to the shelter's residents.

In New York City, Dr. Mark Dollar is one of a group of health-care professionals willing to carry his share of the huge burden. He sees about twenty-five men, women, and children a day at the Lamb's Clinic near Times Square, where many of the homeless congregate. Such physicians, medical assistants, and nurses have to learn to deliver care in a setting where the traditional tools of modern medicine—hi-tech equipment, bed rest, fluids, even aspirin—are often not available.

There are, of course, many other medical people who care for patients for free. Some serve as medical missionaries in third world countries or as volunteers in impoverished sections of the United States. Others staff free clinics, perform screening examinations in shopping centers, or in other ways help some of the more than 30 million Americans who have no health insurance. The combined value of such voluntary service is great, though no one can place a figure on it.

Still, what is done is not nearly enough, according to leaders in the field. They have recently been urging doctors to renew the ancient traditions and contribute more to the care of the poor. They believe that the majority of doctors today act more out of self-interest and less out of public spirit than in the past. The president of the American Medical Association has said that physicians have a basic duty to care for the poor and the needy in their communities because the taxpayers have subsidized their education. And the editor of the AMA's journal has called on physicians to donate at least fifty hours a year.

Dr. David Hilfiker, a physician who serves the poor in Washington, D.C., knows it is not easy to help. He writes:

> *We know that it does little good to offer a medication when our patient needs a home, a meal, a family, love, money and a thousand other things that we ourselves take for granted. We also confront the limitations of a society that refuses to accept responsibility for its broken ones, and so it is tempting to turn away, offering nothing, sparing ourselves the deep frustration.*

In rural and suburban communities the volunteer ambulance corps has long been a tradition. In recent times, with funds and service shrinking as the economy spiraled downward, the cities, too, saw the growth of volunteer corps to ease the pressure on existing services. In New York City alone, there are forty volunteer ambulance corps, most of them in Brooklyn and Queens. They serve areas where poverty and violence add great strain to the city's already overburdened Emergency Medical Service. Licensed by the state's Department of Health, they fill an important need. The members are so devoted to their mission they often pay for equipment out of their own pockets.

There are also teachers and social workers who make a practice of giving to others less fortunate. And lawyers?

What about them? There is a long-standing tradition of the legal profession to do pro bono work.

What is pro bono work? It is work done for free. It can range from representing a death-row inmate with his appeal, to counseling immigrants on their rights. Or from helping a cultural group buy a building to assisting poor tenants facing evictions.

Many years ago Congress set up the Legal Services Corporation (LSC) to provide funds for legal services to the poor. The local offices of LSC have managed to provide such specialized services to thousands of people in need. They perform probably the most thankless task in the justice system. In New York City, for example, these lawyers handle nearly 70 percent of the cases that go through the city's justice system each year. They carry terribly heavy caseloads. Yet they work for comparatively low wages. In 1990 the average annual pay of a legal services lawyer in the United States was $24,000. It is a salary that big-firm lawyers wouldn't bother to sniff at.

Some law firms offer fellowships to law school graduates to practice public-interest law. The graduates' sponsors are public service organizations that provide legal aid to the poor, the homeless, the disabled, the elderly, and those deprived of civic rights.

The need is great. A nationwide survey of poor families concluded that 80 percent of the legal needs of low-income families are not met. Many of those in the fellowship program find that their experiences make them want to stay in public-service law. "I took up law," says one young woman, "because I want to help people not repre-

A homeless man, David Mooney *(shown in a state prison in Storrs, Connecticut)*, was serving his sentence when a court-appointed public defender, Emanuel Margolis, persuaded the Connecticut State Supreme Court to overturn his conviction on the grounds that his "abode" under an abutment on the Connecticut Thruway was entitled to constitutional rights of privacy, and the search and seizure of his belongings at the abutment site violated the Fourth Amendment. The drawing on the next page shows the pro bono lawyer arguing the case before the court. *(Steve Miller/NYT Pictures; drawing by Estelle T. Margolis)*

sented in society to become effective and learn to use their own strength." Another, a young man, had planned on a career with the Foreign Service. But after working with a Homeless Family Rights Project, he says, "I discovered there was a population of the poor in the United States living as if they were in a little third world country and needing all the help they can get."

One of the fellowship lawyers is Steven Hawkins, who grew up in Ossining, New York, near Sing Sing prison. Sponsored by the NAACP Legal Defense and Educational Fund, he produced a handbook for lawyers on the treatment of blacks by the criminal justice system. He

traveled into small southern communities to examine how that system operates for his own people, the African-Americans. He learned that "the situation of black criminal defendants is still atrocious, with blatant violations of constitutional rights with respect to forced confrontations, denial of basic trial process and discrimination against blacks serving on juries." Hawkins as a teenager showed concern for others in need when he visited and befriended men inside Sing Sing. He won a scholarship to Harvard and tutored neighborhood youngsters in his college years. He also worked with troubled adolescents in a summer youth program and moved to one of Boston's poorest neighborhoods to be more available to those who needed help.

Hundreds of lawyers have shown they are ready to help people with AIDS. They write wills, prepare powers of attorney, draft medical directives—such as "do-not-resuscitate" orders—and handle other issues important to people with AIDS. In New York many lawyers donate their time at legal clinics held by the Gay Men's Health Crisis. If people are too ill to attend, the lawyers make visits to homes or hospitals. In the first seven years of the pro bono work about 2,300 people with AIDS got help from 350 volunteer lawyers. The AIDS crisis has done much to bring out compassion and caring for others—in victims, families, friends, community.

10 Not Just Words

If a rich person sees his brother in need, yet closes his heart against his brother, how can he claim that he loves God? My children, our love should not be just words and talk; it must be true love, which shows itself in action.

—I John 3:17–18

Early in the 1990s, hundreds of students from thirty-nine colleges spent their spring break building homes for people in need. They came to Mississippi to build six houses in partnership with low-income families in the small town of Coahoma, where almost all the housing is substandard. Another group of student volunteers went to Sumter County in South Carolina to help rebuild homes devastated by Hurricane Hugo.

Young people on campuses across the country have

been inspired to do such work by Habitat for Humanity (HFH). The organization has caught the imagination of students "ready to turn our backs on Yuppydom and embrace social activism," as one of them put it. They find that Habitat gives them the chance to do something significant with their lives. By 1990 chapters of Habitat had been formed on more than ninety campuses as students returned from building homes for others, fired up by their experience.

Habitat for Humanity is a nonprofit ecumenical Christian housing organization. But it will build a house for anybody and accept anybody as a volunteer, religious connections or not. Both former president Jimmy Carter and his wife, Rosalind Carter, are among its active construction workers. Habitat has over 1,000 affiliates in the United States, Canada, and Australia, and scores of projects in over fifty developing countries. Its aim is to make it possible for low-income families to live in simple, decent homes and to eliminate substandard housing worldwide.

James Logan was the first Habitat for Humanity homeowner in Milwaukee back in 1985. His was one of six houses that 200 volunteers came together to build. After the construction was completed, he spoke at a devotional service for the volunteers. "When we moved into our Habitat house," he said, "we kept looking for the 'catch' in Habitat." But he came to realize that this was not a program where sponsors suddenly back out, or increase the cost, or use the fine print in the contract to withdraw their support. Nor was it a bureaucratic government deal

Jimmy and Rosalind Carter—the former president and first lady—working on one of the many houses they have helped to build. *(Habitat for Humanity)*

tangled in red tape. The house was really his, he had helped build it, and he was proud of it.

"You are changing the world, one block at a time, one family at a time," Logan shouted with joy to the Habitat group.

Habitat houses are built as a cooperative venture between volunteers and home buyers. People like James Logan are expected to keep up payments on a no-profit, no-interest mortgage. These loans are repaid over a fifteen- to twenty-five-year period, and the money is deposited in a revolving Fund for Humanity, which supports further house construction in the area. Habitat takes no government money, but it accepts other forms of government aid, such as land grants, street repaving, and sewer hookups. Neither race nor religion is a factor when local committees choose families to receive Habitat homes.

Only actual housing need counts, and the family's ability to repay a loan, and its willingness to volunteer time.

It isn't only homes that are built by such means. It's communities, too. For in many projects, hundreds of homes are built in a single area. Families enjoy the comfort and security of their own home and the pride that goes with ownership. But more—they also enjoy the sense of community.

It was Millard Fuller who founded Habitat for Humanity in Georgia in 1976. A native Alabaman and a university graduate, he used his business expertise and drive to become a millionaire by the age of twenty-nine. But as the business prospered, his health, marriage, and integrity suffered. The crisis led him to reexamine his life. He and his wife, Linda, sold all their possessions, gave the money away, and began searching for a new focus for their lives. They found it when they, along with several others, created Habitat for Humanity.

How did Millard Fuller come to this decision? He says:

> *I am a Christian person, fired and motivated by the Christian faith, and I feel that it was divine guidance that caused me to take this step. I feel strongly that material abundance was getting in the way of my family relationships and my spiritual life, and that attachment to material things was what got me into trouble. Giving it all away was a dramatic, radical step, one which society might consider somewhat foolish, but I was raised in the Church and have done a lot of Bible study over the years. The teachings of Jesus are very clear. You cannot serve God and money—you have to choose. . . .*

Everybody can be great, because everybody can serve.

—Martin Luther King, Jr.

> *My goals and motivations have changed. Instead of business, I am just pursuing the common good. As Dr. Martin Luther King said, we all should work toward the establishment of the beloved community. Jesus taught us to pray, "Thy kingdom come, thy will be done on earth as it is in heaven." If you work for the coming of the beloved community, you have to be as concerned about your neighbors as you are about yourself. In order to generate income and services and housing and food and clothing for your neighbors, you must have as much fire in your belly as if you were doing it for yourself.*

The roots of Habitat for Humanity are in the teachings of Christianity. The basis for not charging the poor any interest is Exodus 22:25. "If thou lend money to any of my people that is poor by thee, thou shalt not be to him as a usurer, neither shalt thou lay upon him usury." Another maxim comes from Luke: "Whoever has two shirts must give one to the man who has none, and whoever has food must share it."

What families living in poor housing need is capital, not charity, Habitat asserts. This is why it requires prospective homeowners to work side by side with Habitat

Millard and Linda Fuller, who founded Habitat for Humanity in 1976. By 1994 Habitat had completed 35,000 houses worldwide. *(Habitat for Humanity)*

volunteers on their house or the house of a neighbor. This "sweat equity" they put into their home not only lowers costs but creates a true partnership between Habitat and the homeowner. About 2,000 homes were built or renovated in 1988. By 1996, if plans are fulfilled, Habitat expects to be operating in 2,000 American cities and sixty countries. Volunteers elect to work either in the United States or overseas. Habitat's community spirit triggers a warm response. It has found that people want to measure themselves by something other than money. So they flock into its projects from everywhere, to hammer, drill, saw, paint, tote, fit windows—to build a neighborhood and enrich the human spirit.

The college students who volunteer for Habitat for Humanity are by no means the only ones to demonstrate

By 1994, there were nearly 300 Habitat for Humanity chapters on college campuses. Students gave their time, energy, and skills to help construct, repair, and maintain homes for the needy. *(Habitat for Humanity)*

that not all young people are materialistic and self-absorbed. That canard is given the lie every day by the great variety of caring projects the young contribute to.

Young people join with adults in still other volunteer programs to improve the homes of the poor. Annually now for several years, thousands of volunteers in dozens of cities throughout the country help the needy by painting homes in poor neighborhoods. On one spring Saturday in 1991, for instance, crews in Tampa, Florida, using more than 3,500 volunteers, painted 111 houses. In Minneapolis-St. Paul the Paint-a-Thon drew 9,000 volunteers to give 320 homes new coats of paint. Typically the painting days help those who are sixty-two years of age or older and who live below the poverty line.

In several cities the paint comes free from such corporations as Valspar. A committee selects the homes to be painted and coordinates volunteer decorators who help homeowners choose the colors. Cleaning crews, carpenters, and contractors prepare the homes for painting, and landscapers trim the grounds around the houses so the amateur painters led by professionals on each crew can do the job. As one mayor reports, "It builds a sense of community and helps hundreds of senior citizens who might otherwise be forgotten." A volunteer who has helped paint year after year says, "I believe in people. I haven't given up on the human race yet."

Earlier I mentioned the role of Youth Service America in the 1989 hurricane and earthquake that hit the East and West Coasts. Such young people are now active in 3,000 schools, in 500 colleges, and in fifty state and local youth corps. They work in community-based programs to help solve some of the nation's most pressing social problems. One estimate holds that 250 million hours of public service are performed annually by young people.

Take the tutoring program in San Antonio, Texas, where there had been a high dropout rate of Hispanic students before high school graduation. There, under a YSA affiliate, junior high students are trained to tutor kids in a nearby elementary school who are reading two or more years below grade level.

Nicholas, a third-grader, tutored by Oscar, says:

> *My tutor helps me study and read. If I have problems in definitions he can help me. I learn more, so I can be whatever I want to be. I am learning the words I need for whatever I want to be when I grow up.*

And Oscar, his tutor, says:

> *I help them learn and I learn myself. Some of the things I didn't understand in the third grade, I am really learning now.*

Or listen to Christine, a third-grade student who is being tutored by Albert:

> *He helps me with my spelling and makes me feel comfortable.*

Her tutor, a seventh-grader, feels good about what he does:

> *I come over second period and help them learn spelling, math and reading. I like teaching them. It's eas-*

> *ier than I thought and fun. If you like kids, you want them to learn. I feel like a brother.*

New York Care is another example. It is a YSA affiliate for young working New Yorkers, between the ages of twenty-five and thirty-five. It makes direct community service possible for volunteers with demanding and unpredictable schedules. Those interested in children may teach in a tutoring program, go on outings with kids who live in welfare hotels, visit sick children in hospitals, cuddle babies with AIDS, take kids to the circus or a children's theater. Others care for the elderly by spending a few hours visiting a homebound senior, assisting with grocery shopping, lending a friendly ear, taking nursing home residents to a concert, discussing current events, holding a hand. The volunteers work on projects sponsored by many kinds of organizations—the Children's Aid Society, the city's Human Resources Administration, the Coalition for the Homeless, to name but a few.

In one recent winter these volunteers organized a citywide drive to collect and distribute 10,000 winter coats for children and adults in need. By that time Care's membership had increased to 3,000, who served on nearly 400 team projects. Four teams worked on housing renovation projects on the Lower East Side, and in Brooklyn, fourteen staffed several soup kitchens. All volunteers are given orientation sessions and in-service training. The young men and women work individually or in groups, on weekly, monthly, or onetime projects, such as the weekend when thirty volunteers painted

Jennifer Elias of the City Volunteers Corps of Youth Service America in New York City bringing in food for distribution to the needy. *(Anthony Effinger/Youth Service of America)*

bunks, mowed lawns, and cleaned up a 100-year-old summer camp for inner-city kids.

Ohio is one of many states where a statewide coalition of Youth Service groups has formed. Lana Borders, who teaches in the Groveport Freshman School outside Columbus and directs a student community service program called LINK, hopes to see voluntarism spread to all of the state's 600 school districts. She says, "Young people in the schools and also their teachers could have real opportunities to serve their communities. There could be a recognition by young people and their teachers of what community service can do for their own development—that when you serve you also receive. Learning becomes more dynamic. Lifelong learning could be promoted. It would make for wiser decisions about the future."

What the YSA headquarters in Washington does is to

provide technical and developmental assistance to policy makers on every governmental level, and to school, college, and community programs. It keeps them all posted on what goes on in the field at the same time that it helps in the professional development of men and women who administer youth service programs.

Life is tough when you have no place to live, not enough food to eat, no warm clothes to protect you from winter winds, and no doctor to treat your illness. But you are also badly handicapped if you are unable to read.

About 27 million adult Americans—one in five—is functionally illiterate. That means they can't read well enough to fill out forms, read letters children bring home from school, or take telephone messages, to name just a few of the tasks that define modern life. They lack the skills to cope successfully as worker, parent, and citizen.

Why has this happened? There's no one answer, no single cause to be blamed. Many didn't get the individual help they needed when in school. Many had to quit school early to earn a living. Others came to this country from foreign lands and never got the chance to learn to read and write.

The nonreaders are everywhere, in every community large or small. But so are the people who want to help them. Timothy Bierria is one of them. For years he has devoted his time and energy to providing basic education for disadvantaged adults. A native New Yorker, he earned degrees in psychology and counseling, and moved to Pittsburgh to teach school and serve as counselor for social agencies. In 1979 he joined the Greater Pittsburgh

Literacy Council as one of its first volunteers. After acquiring experience helping adult students master the basics of reading and writing, he went on to train new volunteer tutors. He devoted evenings and Saturdays to workshops he set up in all parts of Allegheny County. By 1990, he had played a role in training more than 500 volunteers. Some of the adult learners have gone on to college or found jobs in the information field and in computer programming.

Even though one in five adults in the United States is illiterate, most people find this hard to believe. They think they've never met anyone who couldn't read because adults who can't read often become very skillful at concealing their problem. Many of us think of nonreaders in a stereotyped fashion—that they're all poor, or African-American, or unemployed. But illiteracy is found among all ages, racial and ethnic groups, and income levels. The majority are white, and over half do have jobs.

What volunteer tutors discover is the human side of the picture: how painful and humiliating it is for an adult not to be able to read, what courage it takes to come in and ask for help. And then the joy and triumph the new readers feel as they master the printed word.

There are many channels for volunteers to work through. Literacy Volunteers of America (LVA) is one example. The only requirement is that you can read and you like to help people. LVA believes that well-trained and supported volunteers can be effective tutors of adults. It uses what is called a "learner-centered approach" and "a whole language philosophy." This simply means that people use their life experience, and knowledge of what makes sense in English, when learning to read and write. Tutoring is done both one-on-one and in small groups.

The approach is flexible. A variety of methods and devices are brought into play that seem best fitted to the learner's abilities, needs, and interests. The goal is to help people become independent readers, writers, and speakers of English. LVA's volunteers range in age from sixteen to sixty and up. They represent a wide range of income levels and occupations. Volunteers commit themselves to at least six months, but many stay on for years.

The effectiveness of such volunteer work is apparent in what the learners say:

> *Today is a good day for me. I have learned what courage is. Courage is learning how to read and write.*
>
> *My teacher is teaching my class with warm heart and interesting materials. I have good classmates from different countries and we have become friends. Friendship is human wealth. It should help peace to spread.*
>
> *When I couldn't read, my destiny was decided by others . . . but now I can read and my destiny is my own.*
>
> *Two years ago I was on welfare, unable to drive, and couldn't even read a story to my kids—and it was because I couldn't read. Now I'm doing something for myself. I feel like I can have bigger dreams—I can be somebody. I'm going all the way.*

> *To break out of the shell, to emerge as a new person—it's a very powerful thing. I've had a chance to spread my wings and see what I can do, and I'd like others to have that opportunity. Literacy is not just reading and writing. . . . It's much more than that.*
>
> *I don't have to go to others for answers. Now I can get them by myself.*

LVA was started by Ruth Colvin in Syracuse, New York, in 1962 to tackle the problem of illiteracy in her home community. It had grown to 350 affiliates nationwide by 1989 and had enrolled nearly 40,000 volunteer tutors to work with about the same number of learners. Now LVA gets funding from businesses, government, charities, foundations, and individuals. New programs have been developed to meet newly understood needs: for Head Start parents, for elderly nonreaders, for people with disabilities, for video uses, for the prison population.

Today several national organizations are joined in the Coalition for Literacy. Its goals are to increase public awareness of adult illiteracy and to generate support for campaigns to overcome it. Few know how universal a problem it is. One out of four adults in the world is illiterate. That's nearly 1 billion people. The great majority are in the developing nations, but it's a critically important problem in industrialized countries as well. Remember the U.S. figure? One out of five adults right here cannot read or write.

Larger and older than LVA is another literacy program also centered in Syracuse. Called Laubach Literacy International (LLI), it was founded in 1955 by Frank C. Laubach, who had been a missionary in the Philippines. Its aim is to enable illiterate adults and older youth to acquire the listening, speaking, writing, and mathematical skills to take full advantage of opportunities in their community and to become active in the improvement of their society.

LLI manages a worldwide network of local literacy programs and serves as the center for research and development of program models, methods, and materials. Today its Literacy Action division works with local programs in forty-five states, giving technical assistance to work in libraries, prisons, and adult basic education centers. It now has 2,000 trainers who work with 80,000 volunteer tutors and program administrators. They reach more than 100,000 learners annually.

Abroad, LLI provides technical assistance and support to 174 local literacy programs in eleven developing nations in Latin America, the Caribbean, Africa, and Asia. It was in the Philippines, in 1930, that Dr. Laubach became deeply concerned about the overwhelming poverty and the injustices suffered by the Maranaos people. He became convinced that the only way they could begin to solve their problems was by learning to read and write in their own language. With a simple education method he devised, they began to master the written and spoken word. Then the newly literate Maranaos eagerly offered to teach their families and their neighbors to read and write. Discovering the great untapped potential of volunteer tutors, Dr. Laubach applied what he had learned to adult literacy programs at home in the United States.

He once made this comment on the transformation an illiterate individual experiences by learning to read:

> *A literate person is not only an illiterate person who has learned to read and write, he is another person. He is different. To promote literacy is to change man's conscience by changing his relation to his environment. It is an undertaking on the same plane as the recognition and incarnation of fundamental human rights.*

If you find ways to put books in the hands of children, you're doing a lot to develop literacy. Ben Proctor is one of the volunteer literacy crusaders trying to convert young TV addicts into lifelong readers. When he was a child in El Paso, Texas, Ben's mother, grandmother, and "very good teachers" nourished his affection for books. He grew up to become an engineer and manager of a steel company. After retiring at age sixty-five, he and his wife, Mary, moved to Georgia and then to Mississippi for a while before returning to his hometown.

In Mississippi the Proctors began to work with local schools. They knew that of every three kids starting school, only one graduates. And one out of five grows up unable to read. Ben volunteered his time to the national Reading Is Fundamental (RIF) program. Based in Washington, D.C., it's a nonprofit group aimed at reaching children with books through a corps of 100,000 volunteers. These men and women have made a difference in the lives of more than two million young people in every state. During its twenty-five years of work, RIF has reached children with 100 million books.

Tutor Dorothy Redman *(left)* and a pupil at work in a program of Literacy Volunteers of America in Danbury, Connecticut. *(Literacy Volunteers of America)*

Ben Proctor volunteered his time to tell administrators, teachers, and parents about RIF and to help those schools that need it to get started on a reading program. Local school and community groups raise the money—by business gifts, bake sales, fairs, etcetera—to buy the children's books from publishers at rock-bottom wholesale prices. Each child gets three books a year in conjunction with a reading program planned and carried out by the school and parents.

Results are remarkable. In the Forest City, Mississippi, schools where the Proctors began their work, the first class who received books each year through the ninth grade showed a 16-percent jump in their SAT scores. (The Scholastic Assessment Test is given to high school students as a basis for college admission.) And the number of students who qualified for the honor roll doubled that year.

In El Paso, the RIF program swiftly climbed from one to five to twenty participating schools, serving 20,000 children. Volunteer committees do most of the RIF work, helped by teachers, librarians, and administrators. The volunteers raise funds, select and distribute the books, and supplement reading promotion activities. The Washington headquarters sends much support material, including a dozen pamphlets full of practical ideas parents can use to help their children become better readers.

The first year Ben Proctor began as a volunteer, he set aside $300 and wound up spending $2,600 of his own money—much of it for gas—traveling around to promote RIF's program. "I'm paying back a debt to the public school system," he said. "Undersized, almost blind in one eye, I don't know what I would have wound up doing if I hadn't got an education." And now, through the efforts of people like the Proctors, millions of children are discovering the joy of reading.

11 To Free, to Educate, to Heal

In Harlem there is an odd place called the Children's Storefront. When it opened its door more than twenty-five years ago, that is what it was, a store. But a store transformed into a private school for neighborhood children. A school where the kids pay no tuition. It was started by Ned O'Gorman, a poet who had won prizes and fellowships for his writing. He was editor of a radical Catholic magazine when a priest challenged him to practice what he preached. So he opened the Children's Storefront.

The school no longer holds classes there; now it has 100 students who work in two buildings on East 129th Street. Its budget of over $1 million is raised through contributions. But its goal is still what it always was: "To free, to educate, and to heal the children who come here," as O'Gorman, now in his early sixties, puts it. When its students finish the eighth grade, they go on to public high schools. O'Gorman, wrote a *New York Times* reporter, "has not changed a world that seems to defy rhyme or reason, but he has made a difference in countless young lives. Omar Bailey, who was studiously poking holes in a piece of cardboard on the sidewalk in front of the Storefront, and who wants to attend Yale and become a scientist; Raheen Jones, who suffers from cerebral palsy and who aspires to be an archeologist . . . and Kyle Baxter, who said that 'because my mother never let me have weapons and I never saw anyone locked up' he hopes to become a policeman."

The school is a small oasis of hope in Harlem. Its staying power is generated by a poet who would write:

> *If a man or a society taints a child's childhood, brutalizes it, strikes it down and corrupts it with fear and bad dreams, then he maims that child forever, and the judgment on that man and that society will be terrible and eternal.*

Men and women like O'Gorman can be found in many places. In Boston, seventy-year-old Maurice White, a bachelor who never had kids, is a volunteer in the Hamilton Elementary School in the Brighton section where he has taught Cambodian children how to count change; helped a shy Russian girl master her first words in English; and got one math-phobic fifth-grader over the hurdle of long division. Four full days a week he comes into the school, and for no pay. It's hard working with children who have learning difficulties, and it doesn't always show results. Even average children are not always easy to reach. But though he may be frustrated and tired some days, White always comes in the next morning.

Volunteers are not limited to the elementary level. At Brighton High School a retired physicist and engineer, Ralph Kodis, in his seventies, helps students with algebra and geometry. They come to him in a corner of the school library, where he tries to open up for them the general principles involved in mathematics.

White and Kodis are among America's growing number of older school volunteers. They do everything from helping the school librarian to teaching the children the three Rs with a computer. Boston alone has 1,500 older volunteers in its schools, and nationwide it's estimated there are between 2 and 4 million people offering their time, their skills, their devotion to helping the schools.

Often it's the teachers themselves who volunteer something extra. On Chicago's South Side, Grace Dawson is principal of the Beethoven Elementary School Mondays through Fridays. But on Saturdays she teaches at the Saturday Free School she founded several years ago. There, any child who needs help gets individual attention from Dawson and her staff of volunteer certified teachers. They work with kids from all the nearby schools. Dawson doesn't believe in waiting for other people to solve the community's problems. "You pitch in yourself to turn things around."

In Washington, the nation's capital, Shirley H. Hopkinson teaches prekindergarten in a school in a working-class neighborhood. When she began several years ago, she found more and more children coming to school badly prepared to learn. They needed extra care and resources. She began trying to shore up their lives so that they could move on up in elementary school, ready to learn.

To counter the sad effects of drugs and divorce on children, she began to hold monthly sessions for their parents. They meet at the school from 6:00 to 9:00 P.M. Dr. Hopkinson provides a doctor, a nutritionist, and a school nurse, who donate their time to teach parents the basics of health and to help them see the link between health and intellectual ability. While the parents eat a potluck supper prepared by Dr. Hopkinson, they talk about how important it is that children continue to read and write at home.

Dr. Hopkinson acts as surrogate parent to her pupils as well as concerned listener to their parents. She creates her own lesson plans for each particular class and makes or buys props for teaching tools. It takes a lot of work, a lot of hours—sometimes fourteen a day—and a lot of money. She spends about $3,000 a year of her own money to buy books, toys, and supplies. "Teachers like her," said one educator, "are the real heroes of our schools."

There are some people with wealth enough to benefit large numbers of young students. A new kind of education philanthropy began in the early 1980s when Eugene Lang of New York City promised sixty-one sixth-graders, in the East Harlem elementary school he had attended fifty years earlier, that he would pay for their college education if they would stay in school long enough to take

Eugene M. Lang, with school children for whom he founded the I Have a Dream Foundation. Dreamers take part in a year-round program of academic and related support activities, with the ensurance of college opportunity. The school-based program now reaches into public housing projects in many cities. *(E. M. Lang)*

up his offer. Eight years later more than half the original number were studying in public or private colleges. Some who decided not to go to college held jobs he had helped them find. Others did not make it, trapped by drugs, crime, or pregnancy.

The results of his program were so encouraging that Lang set up a foundation to advise other wealthy people who showed interest in following his model. By 1994 there were 157 sponsors in 54 cities who had secured the funds to assure about 12,000 young people that if they graduated high school, their dream of college would come true.

A somewhat different approach was taken independently by a philanthropist in Worcester, Massachusetts. Jacob Hiatt, a Jewish immigrant from Lithuania in 1935, got a master's degree in history from Clark University in Worcester. The cardboard box company he owned made it possible for him to make a $3-million commitment to provide college scholarships to thirty or more top students in the city's high schools.

In Cleveland, Ohio, Jerome Holmes, a black contractor, heard of these programs and worked out one of his own. He proposed a reward-for-success approach to sixth-graders in a rundown neighborhood. He set aside sums for each A grade earned in each course, with lesser sums for Bs and Cs. The money is held in a fund that can be used only for college. Holmes, who was sixty years old when he started the program, came to Cleveland from Montgomery, Alabama, in 1952. He had nothing but the $200 that his mother raised by selling their cow. He had left school in the ninth grade. His company grew to employ over eighty people. But now, he said, raising yourself up by your own bootstraps is hardly possible. "Everything is computer today; you've got to have education."

In Kansas City, Missouri, Ewing Kauffman promised students at Westport High School financial support if they graduated with their classmates and avoided drugs and teenage pregnancy. They would receive this support whether they planned to enter college, a trade school, or a job-training program. In a working-class community, the school embraces about twenty nationalities, with large Hispanic, Asian, and African-American populations.

Kauffman—the retired head of a pharmaceutical manufacturing company—launched Project Choice at his alma mater to cut the school's high dropout rate. The program now reaches about 1,000 boys and girls at Westport and selected students at five high schools in Kansas City, Kansas, as well. Recently 70 percent of students who graduated went on to two- or four-year colleges, whereas only 20 percent in the past had done so.

Many believe that getting children off to a good start at the earliest point in their schooling is the best way to help them. Phil Garvin thought of a unique way to do this. He pays the bills for teacher-parent-student dinners through his TV production company in Denver, Colorado. Garvin gave the Valdez Elementary School $10,000 to enable the six first-grade teachers to take their students and their students' parents to dinner at a restaurant. Few working parents are able to come to teacher-parent conferences in the schools, and when they do, the fifteen-minute sessions are too rushed to be very helpful. At the evening dinners, there's time to talk and for people to get to know each other better.

Garvin wanted to start such communication from the first year the students have homework, to set in motion better understanding between teachers and parents. Teachers learn about the problems of the parents, and the parents begin to see how they can make a difference. How? By making sure the kids have a place to do their homework, by reading with them for just ten minutes every night, by showing them they care about their schooling. In such districts as this, where many parents are recent immigrants or were school dropouts, the social get-together helps bring down the barriers between school and home.

Arlene and Reuben Mark are a couple concerned with helping children with learning disabilities. Several years ago they adopted such a sixth-grade class in New York City, agreeing to pay for the students' tuition at vocational schools or colleges and for the services they would need getting through high school. The Marks arranged for one-on-one tutoring, and their daughter, Lisa, and her friends volunteered to be Big Brothers or Big Sisters to many of the students. When the students reached the age of sixteen, they were given summer jobs at Colgate-Palmolive, where Reuben Mark is the chairman, and also summer sessions with their tutors. Arlene Mark is a school psychologist.

While most of the examples of people caring about young people are drawn from local sources, there is one woman who has become the leading advocate nationally for children's needs. Marian Wright Edelman heads the Washington-based organization, the Children's Defense Fund, which she founded over fifteen years ago. A black woman in her fifties, she grew up in a small and segregated town in South Carolina, where her father was minister of the Shiloh Baptist Church. She was raised on two expectations: that she get an education and that she give service. Doing work for the community was as much a part of her existence as eating and sleeping and going to church. She and her four older brothers and sisters were not shielded from the world. There are problems out

Marion Wright Edelman, head of the Children's Defense Fund, with a group of children that CDF programs are helping. *(Bruce Reedy)*

there, they were told, but you can do something about them. Although the white world said that poor blacks weren't worth much, her family and the church taught Marian and her siblings this was a lie. And despite negative signals from white society, they grew up knowing who they were.

Marian went to Spelman College in Atlanta, a school for black women. In her senior year in 1959 she became deeply involved in the civil rights movement and joined the sit-ins that hit Atlanta, going to jail for violating the segregation laws.

Her experience led her to a career in law, and she won a scholarship to the Yale Law School. On finishing, she went back to the South to open a legal office in Jackson, Mississippi, so that she could support the civil rights campaign. When the Head Start Project was launched in 1965, she worked with others to get a federal grant that created 2,500 jobs in Mississippi and took care of 12,000 children in its first year.

In the struggle to change things in Mississippi, she came to realize that to get anywhere you needed to change federal policy. She moved to Washington and eventually established the Children's Defense Fund (CDF).

National concern about child care had mounted as the facts became alarmingly clear. One-fifth of America's children—12.5 million of them—live in poverty now. The United States ranks seventeenth in the world in the rate of deaths within the first year of life. There has been a vast increase in reported cases of child abuse and child neglect in the last decade. Teenage pregnancy sentences half a million new babies a year to the sad cycle of poverty and neglect.

A few years ago the CDF put together a coalition of 170 national and local organizations in support of the Act for Better Child Care. It is a major bill that would provide an initial outlay of $2.5 billion in federal funds for outside-the-home child care. The day-care issue is no longer thought of as applying only to poor people and blacks. For with 60 percent of the mothers of young children now working—and because they have to—the public sees it as a white middle-class necessity as well. The Act for Better Child Care would stress health and safety standards in federally supported programs, whether functioning through churches, family day-care homes, com-

If you'd like to help children around the world, there are dozens of ways you can volunteer. The following organizations are among those that offer information and advice:

Save the Children
54 Wilton Road
Westport, CT 06880
(203) 221-4000

U.S. Committee for UNICEF
333 East 38th Street
New York, NY 10016
(800) 252-KIDS

Child Welfare League of America
440 First Street NW
Washington, DC 20001
(202) 638-2952

Kids Meeting Kids
380 Riverside Drive, Box 8H
New York, NY 10025
(212) 662-2327

Returned Peace Corps Volunteers of America
1319 F Street NW
Washington, DC 20004
(202) 393-5501

American Red Cross
17th and D Streets NW
Washington, DC 20006
(202) 639-3039

Amigos de las Americas
5618 Star Lane
Houston, TX 77057
(800) 231-7796

Crossroads Africa
475 Riverside Drive
Suite 916
New York, NY 10015
(212) 870-2210

AFS Intercultural Programs
313 East 43rd Street
New York, NY 10017
(800) AFS-INFO

munity-run centers, or private operators. It would also set minimum standards for the ratio of staff and children and for the training of caregivers.

Congress, as of this writing, has yet to adopt the child-care bill or some variant of it. But Marian Wright Edelman is a tireless catalyst for social change. Her concern and the massive lobbying effort she coordinates are sure to make a difference soon for the children dying as a result of poverty every day in our country.

12

We Are Family

Almost as soon as the Berlin Wall came down and Eastern Europe broke free of totalitarianism, the new democratic governments asked the United States to send them Peace Corps volunteers. In Hungary and Poland, their main mission would be to train teachers of English in the language of commerce, which the East Europeans hoped to develop. The volunteers would also provide assistance in small business administration, environmental concerns, and health care.

In 1990 there were 6,200 Peace Corps volunteers serving in sixty-six countries, working on grassroots, self-help development projects. The Peace Corps, started under President John F. Kennedy in 1961, gathers volunteers to share their skills and energies with people in the developing world. They help others learn new ways to fight hunger, disease, and poverty. In return, volunteers get a new perspective on themselves, their country, and the world.

Nearly 125,000 Americans have volunteered for the Corps. At the invitation of host governments, they have served in ninety-nine countries where they live and work directly with the poeple. When they return home after two years of service, they bring with them an intimate knowledge of other peoples and cultures. And in sharing that information with other Americans, they help shape a broader worldview.

Abroad, the volunteers work side by side with host country coworkers. Together they try to make things happen, useful and lasting things. The projects are determined by the communities themselves. Whatever technology is used has to be affordable and ecologically sound. The aim is to benefit the country while preserving local traditions and values.

The first volunteer to go on duty with the Peace Corps in 1961 was Tom Livingston of Wood Dale, Illinois. He taught English at a high school in Ghana. By the end of that year Corps programs had started in Brazil, Chile, Colombia, India, Malaysia, Nigeria, Pakistan, Philippines, St. Lucia, Sierra Leone, Tanzania, and Thailand.

What it is like to be a volunteer is expressed in letters from someone who recently completed three years of work in Niger. The country is in the Sahara region of West Africa and has a population of about 7 million. The volunteer lived in a tiny isolated village on the edge of the desert, in a mud hut with a Tuareg family. He worked closely with the people of the community, learning their languages.

Here is a typical day:

Peace Corps volunteers are found in every corner of the globe. The photographs above and on the following pages are but a small sample of their diverse activities. Malinda Bjaaland of Whidby Island, Washington, *(top),* teaches English at an elementary school in Pecs, Hungary. *(Paul Conklin/Peace Corps)* Rebecca Enns of Reedley, California, serves as an urban planner in Pokhara, Nepal. She is working with Krishna Panday to plan a botanical garden. *(Bill Strassberger/Peace Corps)*

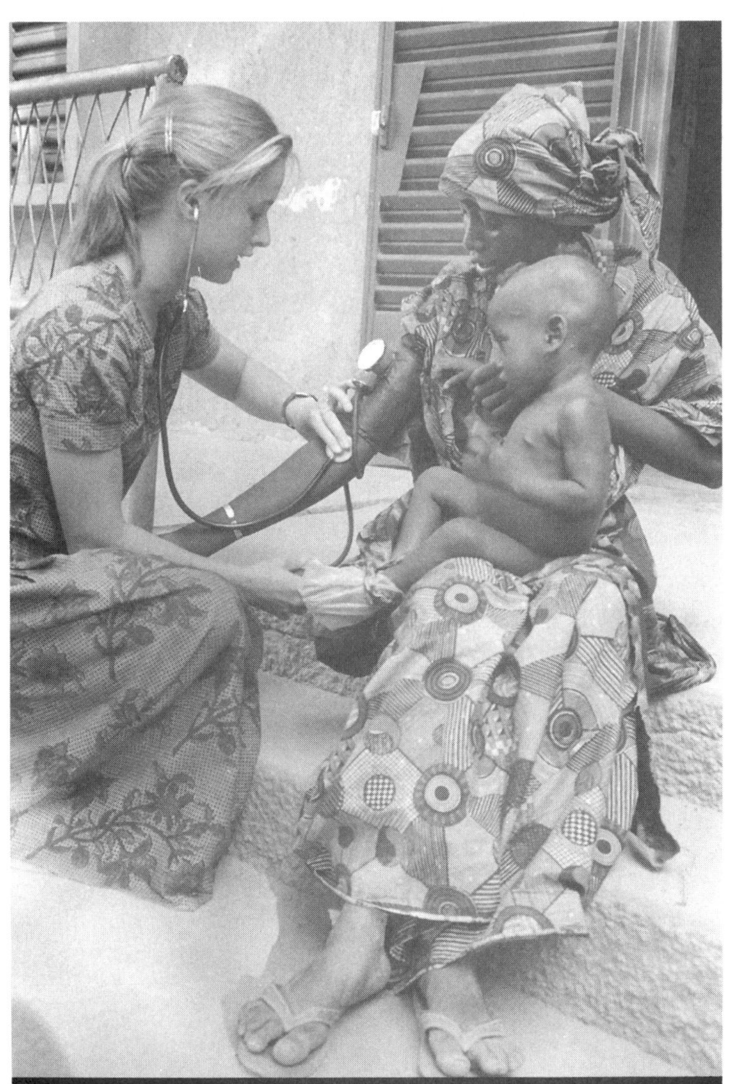

Janet Rich of Hudson, Ohio, works at the mother-child health clinic of Torodi, Nigeria, weighing babies, distributing food, checking blood pressure of expectant mothers, advising mothers on recuperative measures for malnourished children, and in general providing health education. *(Carolyn Watson/Peace Corps)*

Carla Moschetti of Chula Vista, California, teaches team play and exercising as part of her work in youth development in the primary schools around Quetzaltenango, Guatemala. *(Bill Strassberger/Peace Corps)*

Antoinette Fraser of Long Branch, New Jersey, *(top)*, is a special education teacher in Quesada, Costa Rica. *(Paul Conklin/Peace Corps)* Melinda Wyssink works in the Rural Community Development program in Gumine, Papua New Guinea. Here she helps a local family to construct and operate a greenhouse, which will be used in the production of vegetable seedlings. *(Carolyn Watson/Peace Corps)*

I am usually up with the call to prayer—between 5:30 and 6 AM—so that I can go running and exercise before it gets hot. After running, I take a bucket bath, water my garden and eat breakfast. Breakfast usually consists of coffee and fried cowpea cakes. At 7:30, I walk to the nursery. The walk can take anywhere from 10 to 45 minutes, depending on how many people I stop to talk to. Greeting people and exchanging small talk is an important ritual here.

Once I get to the nursery, I usually spend half an hour greeting the farmers I work with and talking about the weather, crops, families, world news. We try to start work by 8:30 or 9, transplanting seedlings. Everyone tells stories and jokes as we work. My newest interest is Housa (a dominant language in this part of Africa) tongue twisters. The farmers get a real kick out of hearing me practice.

Around one o'clock we stop work for siesta. Some days I go home and eat with my family and drink Tuareg tea. Other days I eat with Adamou at the nursery. Work starts again at 3:30 and goes on until 6:30 or 7. In the evening I water the trees in my yard and help the kids at my house fix dinner. We normally eat rice and beans or rice and sauce with a salad. After dinner I sit around with the family, learning Thomasheq (the Tuareg language), telling stories or teaching the young kids French. Later on I read, write in my journal and go to bed, usually at 10 to 10:30.

He describes the people he encounters:

It is amazing to see these people—I would say they are much like the pre-1800 American Indians as far as their westernization goes—meeting the 20th century head-on. The Zormas and Housas are sedentary farmers, while the Tauregs and Fulani are nomadic herders. They wear purple or black clothing, carry a herder's stick, and sometimes wear knicker-type pants. The Fulani have a much lighter pigmentation and almost Caucasian features. Their women wear about 10 huge hoop earrings in each ear and have what we think of as "punk-rock" hairdos.

All of them seem to carry everything on their heads, including not so small tables for selling food. The Niger equivalent of a coffee shop is a man with a 4-by-4 plywood table selling hot Nescafé with milk and sugar and bread. The vendor carries his shop around on his head and his self-contained wood stove/hot-water pot in one hand.

Why do they volunteer?

Dennis Drake, who served in the Philippines, offers his answer:

My first introduction to the Corps was via a television advertisment that ran under the slogan, "The toughest job you'll ever love." Perhaps it was partly the slogan that got me thinking about joining or just the chance to change my life and help people at the same time. Really a simplistic view but maybe common thinking for more than just a few volunteers. Just imagine a person thinking he can actually do something about world hunger, poverty, illiteracy, or disease. Those are not "just" problems, but problems the size of mountains, yet the average Peace Corps

> *Volunteer believes he can do his part by chipping away at those mountains . . . one person at a time.*

Paraguay was the country where Kathleen Maria Sloop served. She writes:

> *At the time I received my assignment from Washington, I had just been promoted to a great position as a market analyst in the bank at which I was working. I was a recent college graduate, so it was hard to give up all the things I had recently acquired, like a car, a good job, a nice house that I was sharing with two roommates whom I loved. But, I also knew that I'd learn more as a PCV, [Peace Corps Volunteer], and I'd be "richer" as a person, if I lived and ate and shared with people who needed my help and friendship. I saw I was easily slipping into the easy, yet sometimes empty, materialistic life we Americans lead. I wanted to do something that would remind me for the rest of my life that Americans' lifestyles are* atypical, *not the norm in the world. It was hard to give up the convenience and comfort of the U.S., and I won't say there haven't been times when I wished I could blink and be home again, but I've also never regretted making the decision I did to serve.*

William Henry Allen was a PCV in Honduras and Colombia, serving four terms:

> *My friends all thought it was a bad idea for me to leave my accounting career behind . . . to go off to some "banana republic" and hard life without modern conveniences.*
>
> *But I was at the time of life when I needed some-*

thing more in my life than "getting and spending." It was time to plow back some of the help others had given me along the way—to do some "good works" of my own in the world. . . . I don't know where I would be today had I not been accepted as a volunteer. But I'm sure life could not possibly have been so interesting. I was not really a happy person before my first tour in Honduras, and I know ever since my life has had meaning.

And what about the people whose home countries the PCVs come to serve in? Mr. Prakong is a fish farmer living in Monsratok, Thailand. He tells what the PCVs meant to him:

Volunteers have helped me a lot in two different ways: first, with their labor, helping me to run the farm—just proving that they are willing to "get their feet wet" alongside me. They dress in jeans, they put on "farmer pants," sometimes they get diseases or infections, but that's the way they work.

The other way they help is that Volunteers know something about how to raise fish, the different species, what feeds they need. I never knew anything like that before Volunteers came. They taught me induced fish-spawning techniques, they helped me build signs on the road to market my fish. . . . Before the Volunteers came, I was a "blind man" in terms of fish breeding. . . . If I had to rely on government administrations, I would be starving by now. They work from the top down, they are eager to show off their technical expertise, but they don't know the faces of the people they want to instruct. Peace Corps Volunteers work from the bottom up. They

> *have the theory, but they are not afraid to get their feet wet, to work one-on-one with the farmers. . . .*
>
> *Working this way with Volunteers, a very close relationship develops. I am the "older brother," the Volunteer is the "younger brother or sister." We suffer the same problems together, we sit together, we eat together—sometimes don't eat together if there's no food-joke together. We are family. I cried when the last volunteer left. I will cry when Ron Rice (my Volunteer coworker) leaves.*

More than ever before, American are offering their skills, their energy, their heart to help people overseas. Proof? In 1992 over 17,000 people applied for the Corps—a greater number than at any time in the past.

13 None of Us Could Exist Alone

So people do care.

The men, the women, the young, the old, all of them are capable of acts of altruism.

They think not only of themselves but of those who need help. And they are willing to give their time, their energy, their skills, their experience, their love, and yes, even their lives, to help others. What they do is evidence that there is more to human nature than selfishness. We are far too likely to accept the dogma that people act only out of self-interest. Knowing more about behavior that transcends the self makes us see how false that view of human nature is.

And perhaps knowing more about altruism will encourage us to build a more caring society. There is evil in the world; we know that. During World War II the horror of the Holocaust happened. Six million Jews were murdered by Hitler's Nazis and their followers in Europe. But

Perhaps there are no greater examples of people who care than those who rescued Jews during the Holocaust of World War II. They were to be found in every country of Nazi-occupied Europe. Oskar Schindler, now well known because of the immense audiences that saw the film *Schindler's List,* is shown here in 1946 *(second from right),* with Mandi Rosner, Edmund Horowitz, Ludmila Pfefferberg-Page, Halinka Horowitz, and Olek Rosner—seven of the 1,200 people he saved. *(Professor Leopold Pfefferberg-Page, courtesy of the United States Holocaust Memorial Museum)*

thousands of Jews were saved from the Nazis by non-Jewish rescuers. By people who care. Those rescuers were not giants walking the earth, not angels, not mythic heroes and heroines. They were "ordinary people"—farmers, mechanics, teachers, merchants, parents, children. Still, they were different from the bystanders who did not help Hitler's victims. Why? In what way?

Among those rescued was young Samuel Oliner, born in a Polish ghetto. Now a sociologist at Humboldt State University in California, Professor Oliner and his wife,

Henny Kalkstein of the Netherlands *(top)* with her rescuer, Dieuke Hofstede, and Dieuke's two sons, Maaike and Andries. *(bottom)* Victor and Josephine Guicherd *(back right)* with the children they rescued in Doullens, France—Betty Lewkowitz *(front, second from left)* and her brother Jacques *(front right)*. After liberation, they were found by their father. Their mother and younger brother died in the Auschwitz death camp.

Pearl, have completed a massive study to find out what led the few to help save Jews, and the differences between the rescuers and the others who might have helped but chose to look the other way. Their staff interviewed over 700 rescuers and nonrescuers living in Poland, France, Germany, the Netherlands, and Italy during the Nazi occupation of Europe.

The Oliners wanted to find out if there is something that can be called an "altruistic" personality. That is, "a relatively enduring predisposition to act selflessly on behalf of others, which develops early in life."

To that end, they explored what various theories about human behavior have had to say about acts of altruism. The approach of the Oliner group takes in both psychological processes and social influences. Behavior, they say, is best explained as a result of the interaction between the two. What the individual is like—his or her internal makeup—interacts with that person's environment. The two influence each other. The nature of your personality and the values you hold mesh with the immediate social situation you find yourself in. That setting is often one over which you have no control, but nevertheless it affects the decisions you make.

Does the personality that develops in infancy remain the same over a lifetime? Most psychologists until recently believed it did. A personality is formed early, they held, with childhood the determining factor in shaping it. And though changes occur, the personality remains pretty steady from that time on.

But other researchers maintain that change in personality goes on throughout life, from birth to old age. They find that we vary considerably in our course of development because of the particular conditions we meet and the experiences we have. So rather than settle on early childhood as the key period for shaping personality, they maintain that any period in the span of life can be a time for critical change. "The emerging view," say the Oliners, "is something of a compromise—yes, some things change and some things remain the same."

Psychologists have studied some groups of people over a long period of time, taking measurements of the same people at different stages in their life. The results have shown that by the time we become young adults, the elements of our personality have achieved a basic consistency. Our values, our preferences in work, our mental well-being, whether we're introverts or extroverts, our openness to experience, and other traits appear to change very little after the early twenties.

The Oliners assert these longitudinal studies are too few in number and too varying in method to call their findings conclusive. Nevertheless, the findings indicate that we are predisposed to certain kinds of behavior even as the years roll on and external circumstances change. "Thus," say the Oliners, "when we say that someone has an 'altruistic personality,' it means not that he or she always acts altruistically but that this person is more likely than others to make altruistic decisions."

Why more likely? How do you develop into such a caring person?

There's no formula for it. But in their study of rescuers,

Marthe De Smet, of Dilbeek, Belgium, with the three Jewish girls the De Smet family hid during the war. On the left is Yvette Lerner, on Mrs. De Smet's lap is Liliane Klein, and on the right is Regine Monk.

the Oliner team observed certain ways such people were raised that help to explain their altruism. It begins with a close family life. Children saw their mothers and fathers behave in caring ways. Parents were not rigid or harsh in discipline but tended toward leniency. They explained to their children why some behavior is wrong, often by making clear how it hurt others. They rarely used physical punishment. And they almost never struck out at their children just to relieve their own feeling of anger or frustration that had nothing to do with their children's behavior.

Parents set high standards they expected their children to meet. Especially in caring for others. Directly or indirectly they let their children know there was an obligation to help others. And to help others in a spirit of generosity, not because you expected a reward or them to do the same for you. Children could see their parents behave in this way, not only toward the children but toward other members of the family and toward neighbors.

Children thus come to value being dependable, responsible, and self-reliant. They see that these qualities help you take care of yourself as well as others. If they experience some failures, it's taken as a learning experience, not as proof that they're bad or stupid or inept.

Growing up that way, these children learn to trust those around them. Their own solid and warm family life makes them ready to form intimate relationships outside the family. Believing that closeness to others, not status, is what makes life good, they choose their friends out of affection, not because of their social class, their religion, or their ethnicity. They feel more at ease with people different from themselves and look for the things that bind them to others rather than the differences that could separate them. The risks they overcome strengthen their ability to confront new challenges. They get to feel their power to influence the world around them.

So it was no accident, say the Oliners, that when the lives of the Jewish outsiders were threatened during the Holocaust, the Christian rescuers with this kind of personal history were more likely to offer help. And so it would be with the many other kinds of caring this book has described. Whether it be heroically attempting to save lives at the risk of losing your own, or simply volunteering to help in the countless ways the world provides, this kind of upbringing may well have played a part.

Many experts besides the Oliners point to the importance of the parental home in developing a sense of moral and social responsibility. But parents alone should not be expected to nurture altruism in their children. It is a community responsibility, too. And the schools—the one institution where young people spend the largest part of their growing-up years—ought to share in that development. They need to do more than teach students the academic skills; they need to help them understand the ways in which they are bound to all humanity.

How? The Oliners again:

> *Schools need to become caring institutions—institutions in which students, teachers, bus drivers, prin-*

> *cipals and all others receive positive affirmation for kindness, empathy, and concern. Participants need opportunities to work and have fun together, develop intimacies, and share successes and pain. Students also need opportunities to consider broad universal principles that relate to justice and care in matters of public concern. Discussions should focus on the logic and values, implications and consequences of public actions, as well as the philosophical heritage that underlies these principles. In short, caring schools will acknowledge diversity on the road to moral concern. They will involve emotion and intellect in the service of responsibility and caring.*

In several places in this book we saw how young people reach out to help others. Yet all too often adults think of young people as burdens on society. The negative stories played up by the media about dropouts, teenage pregnancy, drugs, alcoholism, and crime inevitably contribute to this view. But many projects on the local level show that boys and girls can be tremendous assets to society rather than burdens. As we've seen, places that provide important public services—day-care centers, schools, parks, playgrounds, old-age homes, libraries, museums, hospitals, shelters for the homeless—welcome dedicated people. A national study made by the Commission on Resources for Youth found that programs to develop the potential of volunteer manpower are "increasingly focusing on what is probably the largest, the most zestful and the most under-used manpower pool of all—the nation's youth."

The commission, made up of educators, social scientists, judges, and business leaders, suggested that schools include in their curriculum community service by the students, with credit given for work well done. By "community service" we mean volunteering to tutor others, to work in food banks or shelters for the homeless, in adult literacy programs, nursing homes or hospitals, and such programs as Big Brothers/Big Sisters of America. Such community service would be an ideal way to develop the sense of caring for others and the skills with which to do it. And young people get to feel valued by the community.

Another study of young people, made by the Grant Commission in 1985, held that "if the service commitment begins early enough and continues into adulthood, participatory citizenship would become 'habits of the heart.' " A tradition would be built up to sustain the individual, the community, and the nation.

Hundreds of colleges are now involved in volunteer community service. In Detroit, high school students need to volunteer 200 hours of community service for graduation. Atlanta requires seventy-five hours, while in Springfield, Massachusetts, service is now part of the curriculum from kindergarten through high school. So widespread has the movement become that Republicans joined with Democrats in Congress in the Community Service Act of 1990 to provide a mechanism for the federal funding of service projects through public schools and volunteer organizations.

Many student volunteers not only enjoy the experi-

Young volunteers in the Job Training Partnership program, learning to work with the elderly at a nursing home in Mason City, Iowa. *(Youth Service of America)*

In a Youth Action Council project in Washington, D.C., boys and girls clean up an empty lot. *(Youth Action Council)*

ence but speak of how much they gained from it in understanding the lives of others. Within the schools themselves there are many ways to help others: Students tutor younger children or one another, or shoulder tasks that improve the way their classrooms and their school functions.

In 1992 Maryland became the first state in the nation to require public high school students to perform community service to graduate. The plan calls for students to complete seventy-five hours of community service. Its aim is to teach students the value of citizenship and to encourage them to become contributing members of society.

Regrettably, most schools and colleges still promote competitiveness. You must do your best to beat out everyone else, they urge, not only in sports but in learning itself. Competition is justified as the best way to promote achievement. But is it? Many studies show that cooperative learning procedures are at least as effective. And even more effective in the teaching of disadvantaged, underachieving minority children.

Besides, cooperation makes students feel better about themselves, about their partners in the activities shared, and about other people in general. Schools *can* care about students and help them care about themselves and others.

If people do care, they care, many scientists believe, because they were born to do so. Our very biology endows us with the capacity to care. The human infant is born completely helpless (uniquely so among animals).

Whereas a newborn foal, for example, comes out of the mare and almost at once runs off, a human baby cannot even walk, let alone run from danger or fight it off. Human helplessness lasts for a very long time. Given this extended dependency period, our species couldn't survive without a built-in caring tendency.

But even with this caring capacity, some people still abuse, mistreat, neglect, and desert their children. Why? How can this happen? Psychiatrist Willard Gaylin explains:

> *Because this extraordinary, wonderful, terrifying creature,* homo sapiens *. . . is unique among all creatures. There's a wonderful Talmudic quotation which, in a sense, says that if God had intended man to be circumcised, why didn't he make him that way in the first place? And the answer, with the wisdom of the sages, is that man alone among creatures is created incomplete, with the privilege of sharing with his Maker in his own design. And that is true. Of all the animals, we are the one least dictated to by genetics or by nature. And we have the capacity to shape ourselves for good, or for evil. So that, while we are endowed with certain caring features, we can create a corrupt human being, we can create a corrupt race of human beings and eventually destroy ourselves. Because we are incomplete, we have the capacity—through the way we're brought up, through the way we're raised, through the way we're treated—to become that which we choose . . . or even that which we do not choose, that which we're made of.*

Good—and evil. The struggle between them has been the heart of stories that have fascinated us since the beginnings of history. Built into most of us is an urge to behave decently despite all temptation. But how do we tell good from evil, right from wrong, justice from injustice? Is there some set of ethical principles that are universal? Studies of how children develop in many countries would seem to indicate that there are. In places as diverse as the United States, Great Britain, Mexico, Turkey, Taiwan, and Malaysia children show a latent capacity to evolve along altruistic or ethical lines. They move toward acceptance of two principles known to humanity since the time they were first set forth in the ancient scriptures, according to Dr. Nathan Talbot, of Harvard University. "The first," he writes, "holds that human beings should strive for goals which transcend their own personal, selfish interests. And the second maxim implies that we should be as concerned for the well-being of our fellow man as we are for our own."

Once, when a princess asked the French philosopher René Descartes what the rules of conduct are, he replied, "Although each of us is a person distinguished from all others we must always remember that none of us could exist alone. . . . The interests of the whole, of which each of us is a part, must always be preferred to those of our individual personality."

All this has much to do with our understanding of what democracy is. It promises life, liberty, and the pursuit of happiness. But the chance to be successful in a job or career isn't everything. Citizenship also obliges us to help make the country a better place for all. While democracy offers rights and opportunities, it expects us to fulfill our duty of service to the community.

Giving, through service, is part of the democratic compact. Our form of government depends on people's ability to balance their concern for personal rights with a concern for the rights and needs of others. Can the "Me Generation" become the "We Generation"?

It's happening. Listen to what young people offering their service have to say:

Carlos Bennett, a high school dropout in Brooklyn, after completing a year in the New York Conservation Corps: "After the first month, I saw the work was fun and challenging. I got attached to the Corps. I was helping beautify New York City. I was doing things to make things better in the city."

Or Teresa Duffy, who drives many miles each day to serve in a project with the Wisconsin Conservation Corps: "My family thought it was strange because it is a one-hour trip each way. Working with the Wisconsin Corps has changed me. It has opened me up. I've learned so much."

And Elane Rankin, a Georgetown University student volunteer: "In class, we study the big questions. In the homeless shelter, we live the big questions."

If You Want to Volunteer . . .

This annotated list of resource centers serving young people who wish to do volunteer work is taken from *Choosing to Participate* and is used with the kind permission of the publisher:

COOL, The Campus Outreach Opportunity League, a nationwide campus-based organization, provides college students with the resources and channels for their idealistic energy and creativity. COOL is committed to issues such as literacy, hunger and homelessness, integration, leadership training, publications that help students organize and develop programs, and much more. The COOL National Office is located at 386 McNeal Hall, University of Minnesota, St. Paul, MN 55108. (612) 624-3018

VIA, Volunteers in Action, is Rhode Island's central referral, training, informational, and placement organization for volunteers. VIA services organizations as well as individuals. Whether it is an organization needing to develop a volunteer program or an individual desiring counseling about voluntarism, VIA can help. VIA is located at 229 Waterman Street, Providence, RI 02906. (401) 421-6547

City Year—an urban Peace Corps—is a conservation and service organization that promotes national service at the grassroots level. City Year is represented by high school and college students, twenty-five towns and neighborhoods in the Boston area, and a variety of races, ethnic backgrounds, and socioeconomic levels. City Year is located at 120 Tremont Street, Suite 201, Boston, MA 02108. (617) 451-0699

VAC, Voluntary Action Center of United Way, is an organization committed to the promotion of voluntarism. It identifies a community's needs, recruits volunteers and refers them, as well as providing training and networking opportunities for volunteer directors. VAC is located at 402 Ordean Building, Duluth, MN 55802. (218) 726-4776

Heifer Project International, a nonprofit ecumenical agency, is a learning and livestock center dedicated to the concept of helping people to help themselves and others. HPI works with small groups of farmers in needy places and gives them livestock and appropriate training in order that they may have sufficient food and income. As part of the HPI agreement recipients "pass on the gift"; recipients become donors by passing on livestock or knowledge to their neighbors. Volunteers over eighteen are welcome. HPI is located at P.O.B. 808, Little Rock, AR 72203. (1-800) 422-0474

The Thomas Jefferson Forum, Inc., is a statewide volunteer movement organized to promote high school student involvement in community service. The Forum assists faculty coordinators, at member schools, in developing their own programs designed to recruit students for volunteer work at human service agencies. The Forum is located at 131 State Street, Suite 305, Boston, MA 02109. (617) 523-6699

Youth Service America is an advocate and national nerve center for youth service programs (ages seventeen to twenty-four) across the country. YSA seeks to strengthen collaborative relationships with organizations in the youth service field. YSA provides affiliates with networking, public relations, information sharing, legislative updates, and fund-raising sources and strategies. YSA is located at 810 18th Street NW, Suite 705, Washington, DC 20006. (202) 783-8855

JFK Library Corps, a special JFK Library Foundation program, provides the resources, supervision, and encouragement for young people to make a difference. Corps members decide what projects are worthwhile and how they should be accomplished and then go out and accomplish them. Projects include working in shelters, assisting special-needs teens, and clean-up projects. JFK Library Corps is located at JFK Library Foundation, Columbia Point, Boston, MA 02125. (617) 436-9986

CRF, Constitutional Rights Foundation, seeks to instill in the nation's youth an understanding of citizenship through the values expressed in the Constitution and its Bill of Rights. A wide range of law-related, business, citizenship, and youth leadership programs and publications emphasize challenging content and student interaction and involvement in the classroom, school, and community. CRF is located at 601 South Kingsley Drive, Los Angeles, CA 90005. (213) 487-5590

NDF, Next Door Foundation, is a private nonprofit organization dedicated, thorough various programs, to enriching young lives and bringing them new meaning, structure, and direction. Some of NDF's programs include Early On Home Start, which provides assistance to families with children from birth through five years of age. ABE/GED provides support to young parents who are interested in education, and the Teen Parent Program. NDF is located at 3046 West Wisconsin Avenue, Milwaukee, WI 53208. (414) 931-7708

Youth Resources Center, Inc., is an organization committed to helping runaway, homeless, and other troubled youth. It operates two main programs. Second Mile is a crisis and emergency shelter that offers shelter and counseling. Starting Over provides a positive residential environment where formal training and experience build the knowledge and skills necessary in becoming self-sufficient. Volunteers are placed in a variety of available positions. YRS is located at 7300 New Hampshire Avenue, Hyattsville, MD 20912. (301) 270-3102

Latching on to the many kinds of volunteer programs is a new federal measure adopted by Congress in September 1993. Called the National and Community Service Act, it paves the way for about 100,000 people to serve their communities and pay for college for the next three years. It was the fulfillment of a promise by President Bill Clinton to create a kind of domestic Peace Corps. While not limited to young people, the education financing in the act was expected to be especially attractive to them. The law enables volunteers to receive $4,725—for college tuition, job training, or to pay off existing educational loans—in return for every twelve months or 1,700 hours of service. They may participate for up to two years and receive a maximum of $9,450. Public service advocates hoped the corps would encourage a work ethic and enlarge the pool of volunteers.

Source Notes

The idea for this book was suggested by my wife. You've written so much about people in trouble, she said, and often about those who've tried to overcome or remove those troubles. But isn't there room for a book devoted to altruism itself? How much of it is there? Within each of us? In the society at large?

A good idea, I thought, and squirreled it away in the file of possible projects. It didn't remain dormant. Once alerted to it, I began to notice examples of altruism mentioned in the media, popping up in conversation, recalled in memory. Yes, there is a book here, I thought.

I began to read systematically the literature on the subject. The references were deeper and more varied than I'd anticipated. (Under Altruism see also Egoism, Helping Behavior, Self-Denial, Self-Interest, Self-Sacrifice . . .) I found that philosophers, psychologists and psychotherapists, sociologists, economists, and historians were having their say, each profession viewing altruism from its own perspective. And each book, as is generally the case, offering a bibliography to steer me to still other sources.

Once I became aware of how extensively altruism is expressed by caring people who volunteer their time and energy and experience, I reached out to the multitude of organizations that both stimulate and channel such efforts. There are thousands of them, and I had to be selective. (I hope those not mentioned will forgive me.) All the organizations I contacted by mail or telephone were very cooperative, sending me reports, brochures, letters, case histories, bulletins, and even books. There is no room to list them all, but the text includes the names of those I finally chose to write about or to quote.

It was hard to get a handle on so abstract-seeming a subject. (Of course it isn't abstract; the evidence of altruism is in the lives of men, women, and children you will find represented in this book.) Eventually connections occurred to me, and the material took shape. For anyone who wishes to pursue the subject further, refer to my bibliography.

Bibliography

Better, Nancy Marx. "Green Teens." *New York Times Magazine*, March 8, 1992.

Bok, Sissela. *Lying: Moral Choices in Public and Private Life*. Vintage, 1979.

Coles, Robert. *The Call of Service: A Witness to Idealism*. Houghton, 1993.

———. *Dorothy Day: A Radical Devotion*. Addison Wesley, 1987.

———. *The Moral Life of Children*. Atlantic Monthly Press, 1986.

Damon, William. *The Moral Child: Nurturing Children's Natural Moral Growth*. Free Press, 1988.

Edwards, Carolyn Pope. *Promoting Social and Moral Development in Young Children*. Teachers College Press, 1986.

Fogelman, Eva. *Conscience and Courage: The Rescuers of the Jews During the Holocaust*. Anchor Doubleday, 1994.

Freedman, Marc. *The Kindness of Strangers: Adult Men-*

tors, Urban Youth, and the New Voluntarism. Jossey-Bass, 1993.

Fuller, Robert C. *Ecology of Care.* Westminster, 1992.

Gaylin, Willard. *Caring.* Avon, 1976.

Gaylin, Willard, Ira Glasser, Steven Marcus, and David Rothman. *Doing Good. The Limits of Benevolence.* Pantheon, 1978.

Gilligan, Carol. "In a Different Voice: Women's Conception of Self and of Morality." *Harvard Educational Review,* vol. 47, no. 4, November 1977.

Goldsmith, Suzanne. *A City Year: On the Streets and in the Neighborhoods With Twelve Young Community Service Volunteers.* The New Press, 1993.

Gouinlock, James, ed. *The Moral Writing of John Dewey.* Hafner, 1976.

Held, Virginia. *Rights and Goods: Justifying Social Action.* Free Press, 1984.

Hoose, Phillip. *It's Our World, Too! Stories of Young People Who Are Making a Difference.* Little, Brown, 1993.

Ignatieff, Michael. *The Needs of Strangers.* Viking, 1984.

James, William. *The Philosophy of William James.* Modern Library, 1925.

Kagan, Jerome, and Sharon Lamb, eds. *The Emergence of Morality in Young Children.* University of Chicago Press, 1987.

Lande, Nathaniel, and Afton Slade. *Stages: Understanding How You Make Your Moral Decisions.* Harper, 1979.

Larrabee, Mary J., ed. *An Ethic of Care.* Routledge, 1993.

Latane, Bibb, and John M. Darley. *The Unresponsive Bystander: Why Doesn't He Help?* Prentice Hall, 1970.

Luks, Allan, with Peggy Payne. *The Healing Power of Doing Good.* Fawcett Columbine, 1992.

Manser, Gordon, and Rosemary Higgins Cass. *Voluntarism at the Crossroads.* Family Service Association, 1976.

Meltzer, Milton. *Rescue: The Story of How Gentiles Saved Jews in the Holocaust.* Harper and Row, 1988.

Mogil, Christopher, and Anne Slepian. *We Gave Away a Fortune.* Philadelphia: New Society, 1992.

Oliner, Samuel P., and Pearl M. Oliner. *The Altruistic Personality.* Free Press, 1988.

Rolzinski, Catharine A. *The Adventure of Adolescence: Middle School Students and Community Service.* Youth Service America, 1990.

Rushton, J. P., and R. M. Sorrentino, eds. *Altruism and Helping Behavior.* Lawrence Erlbaum, 1981.

Staub, Ervin. "Evolution of Caring and Nonaggressive Persons and Societies." *Journal of Social Issues*, vol. 4, no. 2, 1988, pp. 81–100.

Stein, Harry. *Ethics (and Other Liabilities).* St. Martin's, 1982.

Stoskoff, Alan L., and Margaret Stern Strom. *Choosing to Participate: A Cultural Examination of Citizenship in American History.* Facing History and Ourselves, 1990.

Talbott, Nathan. *Raising Children in Modern America.* Little, Brown, 1976.

Thomas, Lewis. *Late Night Thoughts on Listening to Mahler's Ninth Symphony*. Viking, 1983.

Wachtel, Paul L. *The Poverty of Affluence: A Psychological Portrait of the American Way of Life*. New Society, 1989.

Wheelis, Allen. *The Moralist*. Basic, 1973.

Wilson, James Q. *The Moral Sense*. Free Press, 1993.

Wren, C. Gilbert. "Some Things I Have Learned and Some I Am Still Learning." *Journal of Counseling and Development*, vol. 64, October 1985, pp. 99–102.

Zahn-Waxler, Carolyn, E. M. Cummings, and R. Iannotti, eds. *Altruism and Aggression: Biological and Social Origins*. Cambridge University Press, 1986.

Finally, here is a short list of some practical guides to volunteering.

Carroll, Andrew, with Christopher Miller. *Volunteer USA*. Columbine, 1991.

Gilbert, Sara. *Lend a Hand: The How, Where, and Why of Volunteering*. Morrow, 1988.

Hollender, Jeffrey. *How to Make the World a Better Place: A Guide to Doing Good*. Quill-Morrow, 1990.

Javno, John. *Fifty Simple Things Kids Can Do to Save the Earth*. Earthworks Group, 1991.

Kipps, Harriet C., ed. *Volunteerism: The Directory of Organizations, Training, Programs, and Publications*. 3rd ed. Bowker, 1990.

Index

Note: Page numbers in italics refer to photographs.

PENN HIGH SCHOOL
INSTRUCTIONAL MATERIALS CENTER
MISHAWAKA, INDIANA